THE TRAIL OF
Transforming
FAITH

WHEN GOD CALLS YOU TO LEAVE EVERYTHING BEHIND

BOBBY BLANTON

Produced with the assistance of Fluency Organization, Inc. in
Tyler, TX. Design and layout by DK Designs Group.

To Debbie, Delyn, Bobby Greg and Jesalyn…you have enriched my life beyond measure. I'm so grateful that God has placed you into my life! Each of you has been an endless source of encouragement and joy! (Not to mention the illustrations!)

Table of Contents

Foreword

"Abraham went out to a land he knew not where..."
(Hebrews 11:8). What a statement! God said, "GO!" and
Abraham went—and he didn't even ask any questions!
Abraham is rightly called "The Father of the Faith." Ours
is rightly called, not the Christian religion, or Christian
movement, but "The Christian Faith." Faith is indeed
the heart of who we are. Do you want to know the secret
to joy in Christ? Likewise, live every moment with the
humble willingness in your heart that says, "Jesus, the
answer is yes. Now, what's the question?"

     As Pastor Bobby Blanton explains in his book, *The
Trail of Transforming Faith*, our dynamic faith is not so
much believing God can but also believing God will (and
that in God's mind it's already happened!) We must go
forward in faith and simply appropriate what has already

been accomplished. Moses didn't stand on the banks of the Red Sea and say, "If that thing would open up, I'd go forward!" Upon receiving the call from God, Abraham didn't stand there and ask, "Where are we going?" Both men just said, "Let's go!"

The lights don't come on until after you turn the switch. Faith demands our decisive response. And every decisive action in life should be based on trusting not just what God says, though this would be enough, but also on the trustworthiness of what He has proven Himself through our experience to be.

In reading this book, you will hopefully be encouraged like Abraham to willingly say, "Lord, the answer is yes! Now, what is the question?"

Dr. John Bisagno
Pastor Emeritus, First Baptist Church Houston

Houston, Texas
July 2013

From the Author

I have lived a blessed life. I have been given opportunities and extended pleasures and benefits far beyond what anyone should reasonably expect. God has put people into my life who have greatly enriched me—parents, teachers, coaches and friends. There are many who have invested their time and effort into my faith development. Beyond this wide group, there are others that I'd like to acknowledge as making a special contribution to this effort.

I want to thank the members and congregations of three wonderful churches that I have pastored. Macon, Midway and Balfour—God will have a special place in Heaven for you for having to put up with some of the sermons and mistakes that you endured! I want to especially acknowledge my present wonderful church, Lake Norman Baptist. Thank you for calling me to this wonderful area and to your wonderful church. For 16 years, it has been my privilege to journey with you as God has blessed our church. (I'd like to think that I had 16 more years ahead with you, but you and I both know that's not going to happen!)

I want to thank the LNBC staff. I have been blessed to be surrounded by such a great team! Thanks for the many times you have made me look good! Especially to my Ministry Assistant, Sue Beard, thank you for the typing and deciphering of unintelligible scribbling.

I want to thank two other individuals who, in my estimation, helped to push me and make this project a reality. I want to thank Bryce Elliot. Bryce, you have always challenged me in many ways. Writing this book was just one. You convinced me that I could do it. For that, I'll always be grateful.

I want to also thank David Dykes for encouraging me to "enlarge my preaching ministry." David, it was your timely and wise push that sent me over the edge! Thank you!

I want to thank Mary Ann Lackland and Fluency, Inc. for her wise counsel, editorial "adjustments" and for being such a great cheerleader! It was such a joy to work with you!

I also want to acknowledge the many others who have profoundly impacted my life through their preaching/teaching and writing ministries. Among them are Ron Dunn, Gordon MacDonald, David Jeremiah, James Boice, Gene Getz and Kent Hughes. I fully acknowledge that it was these wonderful teachers who shaped my thoughts and ideas on the richness of Abraham. Especially, I would note that it was while reading Gordon MacDonald's book, *Mid-Course Correction*, that the idea for a series of sermons I preached at LNBC was born. It was that series of messages that became the basis for this book.

Introduction

Go with me to a place called Mt. Moriah in the Promised Land. It's not the most beautiful of places. As a matter of fact, it looks rather ordinary. Visually, there is nothing that sets this place apart from the thousands of other mountainous spots surrounding it. However, as you will soon see, this place is different. While there are other more scenic places on earth, I dare say not one at the moment is more sacred.

From a distance, we see an old man busily preparing an altar. On that altar is wood. It's obvious that he intends to lay an offering on that altar for a sacrifice. It also seems obvious that what is about to happen here is an act of worship.

At first, we are struck by the depth of devotion of the old man going about his business. Yet as we zoom in, our initial favorable impression begins to fade. For as we take a closer look, we notice something strange—something barbaric—something too unbelievable for civilized minds. For upon this altar is a young man—his son—bound up and awaiting his awful fate. The whole scene is reminiscent of some ancient pagan ceremonial rite. Now we see the old man, knife in hand, raised to make its fatal blow.

The entire scene is repulsive to us. Who is this man? Is he a pagan worshipper? If so, who is this deity he hopes to appease? What kind of god would require such a sacrifice? Or, is this scene playing out before us just another tragic example of demented and delusional thinking? Tragically, our world has become all too familiar with this type of ugliness.

As we witness this unfolding drama being played out before our eyes, we're not aware of all that has gone into the making of this moment. Well over 100 years and hundreds of miles have led up to this decisive moment. Now as the old man raises his knife, he just as quickly lowers it. Strange. Something has arrested his intentions. A voice has been heard. There, we knew it all along. We knew that behind this bizarre scene must have been someone who "hears voices." Well, here is our evidence. This confirms for us that the old man is some "crazy" who is hearing voices in his head that tell him to kill. We're not surprised. Sadly, it happens in our world every day.

But whose voice *stops* this wretched deed? It isn't a human voice, but it is what author Gordon MacDonald simply refers to as the Voice.[1] Ironically, it

---

1   Gordon MacDonald, *Mid-Course Correction*, Thomas Nelson Publishers, 2005, p. 54.

is the same Voice the old man heard many years earlier that started the whole set of events leading up to this very moment. Only now the Voice calls him by name and halts this barbaric action. "Abraham! Abraham!" the piercing voice roars. "*Now* I know that you fear God." "Now," the implication being that some sort of revelation has just come to light in this unfolding drama. Some accomplishment has been gained that only "now" can be fully appreciated.

Of course, we now recognize this old man. His name is Abraham. And it doesn't escape us that we have been privy to the most sacred of all moments. Before this moment, Abraham's faith may have been certain... but **"Now"** it is crystal clear. Abraham possesses a unique quality of faith that can only be described as "Moriah faith."

The great Michelangelo, when asked how he was able to carve a beautiful angel out of a block of marble, is reported to have said, "I just chip away everything that doesn't look like an angel." Michelangelo began his work with a clear picture of the desired end in mind.

Likewise, we begin our quest of understanding the transformation that Abraham's faith underwent by beginning at the final scene. We begin where Abraham's faith was fully and unquestionably centered upon God. What started out for Abraham as simply "The Voice" has now become so much more. It is said of Abraham that he was a friend of God's. That distinction is given to no one else in Scripture. Maybe it's because no one else pleased God as Abraham did (Hebrews 11:6a). What Abraham displayed in that barren and secluded mountainous setting we are referring to as "Moriah faith." There are two distinct features of Moriah faith.

First, *Moriah faith involves the ability to hear*

the voice of God (22:1). It's hard to fully appreciate this moment without realizing that Abraham came from a culture where people never heard the voice of their god. The gods of Abraham's culture were unmovable, stoic and silent. The fact that Abraham heard the voice of God in that culture of silent gods is nothing less than remarkable. Furthermore, we are wary of people who say they hear voices. Too many whackos have done violent things because they thought they heard voices. As uncomfortable as that may make us feel, it is, nevertheless, a distinctive feature of what makes Abraham the towering faith figure that he is.

I challenge you to consider the importance of hearing the voice of God in your life today. God still speaks, you know. Do you ever hear Him? There are times when we hear Him speak within our spirit as that gentle nudge or reminder. But even then, we must be very cautious. Quite frankly, not everyone has the direct line to God that they would have you believe! However, the voice of God *can* be heard clearly today. In the passage of time since Abraham, the voice of God still speaks. Paul reminds us in Romans 10:17, *"Faith comes from hearing the message and the message is heard through the Word of Christ."* Holy Scripture is God's voice that calls out to us as to Abraham. God, in times past, may have spoken through His prophets, apostles and servants. In careful and meticulous detail, this voice was recorded so that it might be heard in succeeding generations. Want to hear His voice? Commit to a daily, systematic and consistent reading of His Word. There you will hear the voice of God.

Second, *Moriah faith involves the willingness to trust the purpose of God* (22:3-5, 8). There was a time when Abraham would have violently protested what unfolded atop Mt. Moriah. However, Abraham now demonstrates a faith that has been developed over many years of trials and hardships. Now Abraham knows that God can be trusted, even if God must do something never before done. Hebrews 11:17-19 describes it this way: "*By faith Abraham, when God tested him, offered Isaac as a sacrifice. He who had received the promises was about to sacrifice his one and only son, even though God had said to him, 'It is through Isaac that your offspring will be reckoned.' Abraham reasoned that God could raise the dead...*"

Dare I remind us that this was something that God had never done before? There was no previous example that Abraham could point to in which he could rest his faith. Abraham was plotting a new course, a new trail of faith. He was willing to trust the purpose of God, even when that purpose was still hidden within the heart of God. In spite of the lack of outward evidence, Abraham trusted what was sealed within the heart of God. When he could not see the "how" of God, Abraham was willing to trust the "heart" of God.

Moriah faith doesn't try to understand the "how" or "why" of God; we trust Him even when we don't understand. And what is more, we trust Him when our heart is breaking. We will never understand the burden that Abraham carried up the mountain that day. The load he carried far surpassed the weight of wood and supplies. His heart breaking, Abraham had given himself over in obedience to the Voice that now directed his course.

It's hard for us to fully understand what happened here, until we begin to understand all that went into the making of the "Now" of which God spoke (22:12). We must follow a long and winding trail back down that mountain to Ur, the place where it all began. Along the way, it is important that we go back and revisit all the significant moments that made this the moment it was.

We leave Moriah for now. We've seen enough to know how this transformed faith will appear at the end. We now must travel back many miles and many years to where this transforming trail began. Come with me and see the trailhead where Abraham's faith was born and let's follow him along the path as his faith is forged into something that will one day be described as "Moriah faith." In so doing, we will discover that our faith will also be transformed along the way.

CHAPTER 1:

You Want Me to Do *What?*

"The Lord had said to Abram… go to the land I will show you." (Genesis 12:1b)

If a journey of a thousand miles begins with one step, Abraham's first step of faith put him on a trail that changed his destiny and transformed his faith forever. Walking that trail forced him to grow in ways he'd never known before. Abraham wasn't the same man willing to sacrifice his son on the top of Mt. Moriah years later as he was when he was living an ordinary life in Ur. The thousand-mile trail of transformation began for him with one step. He responded to a simple call from God who told him to leave Ur and follow Him to an unknown place that He would "show" him.

We know very little of the details of that call. We can, with good reason, assume there were no flashing lights or loud sirens that accompanied God's call on his life. We don't know how Abraham heard the call; nor do we know under what circumstances that call came. We are simply told, "*The Lord had said to Abram…*" We are left to fill in the blanks.

I'll never forget a night when all our kids were home and the entertainment they chose for the evening was old family videos. Everyone got a kick out of reliving those memories and it was amazing to me to see how much my kids had grown. (Even more amazing was how much hair I seemed to have lost while they were growing!) Of course, I'm grateful that my kids have grown (boy, am I glad!) because growth is a natural part of healthy life.

The same principle of growth applies to our spiritual life. The writers in the New Testament assume growth is a part of life and they challenge us to pursue it. Paul commended the Thessalonian believers for their desire to please God and for the way they loved other believers. And yet, he also urged them to do so "*more and more*" (1 Thessalonians 4:1,10). Likewise, Peter urges us to "*Grow in the grace and knowledge of our Lord and Savior*

Jesus Christ" (2 Peter 3:18).

The lessons Abraham learned in those early, tentative years of following God would carry him all the way to Mt. Moriah. If we want our faith to be transformed from what it "is" to what it "could be," these are the same lessons that we must learn as well.

Willing to Follow God's Voice

Transforming faith begins with a willingness to follow God's voice. The writer of Hebrews in chapter 11 has much to say about Abraham's faith. Just two verses before using Abraham as a model of faith, the writer conveys two important things about faith. First, he reminds us of faith's essential role in our relationship with God. The writer says, "*And without faith it is impossible to please God…*" (v.6). Failing to trust will not result in difficulty, but in impossibility. It's not that my spiritual life will struggle, but it will not even exist! Failing to trust God makes it impossible to please Him. If I tried to jump up and touch the moon, or swim across the Atlantic Ocean, the results would be no less futile than if I attempted to live in relationship with God without this element of trust. Simply put, God derives no pleasure from me if I'm not willing to trust Him.

There is nothing new about this idea of living by faith in relation to God. God has always chosen to relate to humankind through faith. We see this principle clearly in the aftermath of Adam's fall in Genesis 3. God set forth a promise of deliverance that required faith when He said to Satan, "*And I will put enmity between you and the woman, and between your offspring and hers; he will crush your head, and you will strike his heel*" (Genesis 3:15). Here, God promised that one day a deliverer over sin and

Satan would come—the Messiah. Adam would live by faith looking forward to this day. As Christians, we look back to that promise and see that is was Christ and His resurrection that brought defeat to Satan and triumph over death.

Faith Means Believing God Exists

There is a difference between a "faith-centered" faith and a "God-centered" faith. Many people proudly profess their faith, as though this will gain for them whatever results they desire at that moment. But truth be told, they may only have faith in "faith." This is not good enough to qualify for God's pleasure. God requires of us that the object of our faith be Him and not an impersonal process. We must have faith in God alone. But what is "faith" anyway?

The writer of Hebrews helps us to understand a twofold definition of it in Hebrews 11:6. First, "...*anyone who comes to him must believe that he exists...*". Abraham's steadfast belief that God exists made him a man of faith and a "friend of God." When Abraham set out in response to God's voice, he wasn't primarily heading out for a new dwelling place ("the land" that God would show him). Yes, that would come in time. However, the true motivation behind Abraham's departure was his desire to follow the One who beckoned him to leave.

Abraham was not looking to simply change his address. It was much deeper than that. Abraham was following God, and he trusted that God would take him to another land. Hebrews 11:8 says, "*By faith Abraham, when called to go to a place he would later receive as his inheritance, obeyed and went, even though he did not know where he was going.*" Abraham believed that God "existed" in a time and in a place where such belief would have been rare, or even non-existent, because of the polytheistic culture. This is what makes Abraham's faith in a God he barely knew all the more remarkable. He had the confidence that God was there with him in his present moment and that He desired a relationship with him. That's where our faith must begin, too. We must confidently know that God is present in our lives and in our circumstances and that He desires for us to enter into an intimate relationship with Him.

Faith Means Trusting God for His Reward

The latter half of Hebrews 11:6 continues with a second requirement of faith: we must believe "...*that he rewards those who earnestly seek him.*" What was the "reward" Abraham anticipated? It was "the land" and all the blessings that would come with it (Genesis 12:2-3).

The unwillingness to trust God is an assault not just on His existence but also upon His character. Pastor Tony Evans uses a simple definition several times in his book, *Free at Last*.[2] He says that faith is the willingness to live as if what God said is true. A failure to trust God, therefore, is an accusation leveled at the integrity of God. It is the expression of Satan's familiar suggestion, "*You will not surely die...*" when he called God's character into question in Genesis 3:4 after Eve told him what God had said about eating the forbidden fruit.

Faith requires having confidence that God is true to His promises and that He "rewards" those who faithfully trust Him. The witness of my faith should be lived out each day in the confident assurance that God has

2   Tony Evans, *Free at Last: Experiencing True Freedom through Your Identity in Christ*, Moody Publishers, 2005, p.69.

my best interest at heart and that whatever lies ahead, He will take care of it.

As you think about your own life, are you following God with that same degree of confidence? Do you rest in the assurance that He is the one, true God worthy of following…wherever? If I am confident that God is God (and therefore truly worthy of following), then I should also have the confident assurance that He will not only reward me but also that He will reward me with my best interest in mind. Like Abraham, I place my trust in Him who will reward me in His own way and in His own timing. If I start out with my eyes on "the land," I'll be tempted to settle somewhere (anywhere!) before I arrive at the place where God's promises reside. Of course, the longer and harder the trail God leads us along, the more attractive some other "lands" along the way will look. I'll be tempted to settle for less than God's best.

You Want Me to Do *What?*

I couldn't have been any more than six years old at the time. (I'd like to remember it that way, at least. To say I was any older than that would be really embarrassing.) I had gone on and on for weeks about wanting to go to the fire station and slide down the firemen's pole, as I had seen firemen on television do. On this particular occasion, I mentioned it again just as our family was driving past a fire station. The details are a little foggy here (remember, I was just six!), but the next thing I remember is that I was somehow standing in the second floor sleeping unit of the fire station looking down through a "slide-hole." There before me was a shiny brass pole that the firefighters would use to make their quick entry into action near the fire engine below. I remember looking down through that hole and seeing my dad and an unknown fireman. My dad tried coaxing, "Just hold on to the pole and slide down. I'll catch you. No need to be afraid." (Yeah right. Easy for him to say!) All I could think was, "There is no way I'm going to slide down that pole! It's just too risky! What was I thinking?"

It was a long way ride home while I sat quietly in the backseat. My boastful talk had been exposed for what it was—cowardice. Though my dad never brought up the subject, I've often wondered what he must have felt on the drive home. No amount of coaxing or assurance could entice his son to trust him enough to "slide" into his awaiting arms.

Sadly, that embarrassing scenario has been played out many times in my spiritual journey as well. There have been times when I confidently assured God that I could handle a situation, only to have my boastful promises exposed for what they really were: pride. There have been many times when I've chickened out because I just couldn't risk it. It looked too scary. I just couldn't trust God. There have been times when I've contemplated the need to lead into a new, uncharted area of ministry. I've heard God beckon me to "slide down…I'll catch you," but I was too worried about the outcome. There have been times when I should have trusted His Word, but I chose to be a slave to what other people might think of me.

As we prepare for this long and winding trail that transforms our faith, we tend to include unnecessary things in our backpack. These things grow very heavy and pose a great distraction to us. Abraham faced the same challenges, and I suppose things have changed very little over the years.

Faith Distractors

I have heard faith described as a "leap into the dark." That idea has never seemed favorable to me. If I'm not willing to grasp a brass pole that I can clearly see, I'm sure not going to leap into darkness. Fortunately, I don't have to do that. As I've studied the Bible, I don't recall a time when God ever expected anyone to "leap into the dark." God's call to Abraham wasn't into darkness, for God said, *"...I will show you"* (Genesis 12:1). Admittedly, however, there was a lack of details.

One thing that distracts us on the journey of following after God is our need to know all the details of His plan. However, details don't build faith. Details only distract us from faith. Think about Job (another biblical character who showed great faith amid difficulty). What if God had given Job the details for which he yearned as he endured his horrible sufferings? Would the details have made him feel better about what he was experiencing? It's doubtful. Besides, what if Job had wanted to know more details about the details? On and on it would go without end.

I can't help but think about Moses here, too. In Exodus 3-4, the burning bush was a dramatic invitation to expanded service. However, Moses wanted to know the details. And the more Moses knew, the less attractive this tour of duty seemed to grow! Eventually, Moses resisted until God gave him what he was so determined to get—details! He even allowed Moses' brother Aaron to come along for support, but that wouldn't prove to be very smart. Be very careful regarding what you stubbornly ask for because God may actually give it as a judgment against your stubbornness! Sometimes our answered prayers turn out to be our most painful thorns, as Aaron would later become an embarrassment of failed leadership (Exodus 32).

Getting bogged down in the details is the devil's way of casting darkness upon our trail of faith. Satan, though he often *"masquerades as an angel of light"* (2 Corinthians 11:14), is actually an "angel of darkness." Details are often the means whereby Satan keeps us from exercising our faith. Faith is not a "leap into the dark." That's Satan's realm. Faith is a willing step into the light. That's where, and who, God is (1 John 1:5).

The psalmist confidently stated, *"The Lord is my light...whom shall I fear?"* (Psalm 27:1). Isaiah, the famed prophet, once challenged us to *"walk in the light of the Lord"* (Isaiah 2:5). As clear as these statements are, perhaps the clearest are Paul's words in 2 Corinthians 4:4-6: *"The god of this age has blinded the minds of unbelievers, so that they cannot see the light of the gospel of the glory of Christ, who is the image of God...For God, who said, 'Let light shine out of darkness,' made his light shine in our hearts to give us the light of the knowledge of the glory of God in the face of Christ."*

Given the light of God's revealed Word through Christ and the New Testament, our walk of faith is much easier than it was for Abraham (or Moses, or Job). We have the light of God's full revelation in Christ and the insights of His Apostles. We also have over 2000 years of reliable testimony of God's faithfulness to His people. Abraham had none of these. He simply had a "Voice" calling to him. And in spite of such limitations, *"...Abraham, when called to go to a place he would later receive as his inheritance, obeyed and went, even though he did not know where he was going"* (Hebrews 11:8).

Do It Anyway!

Another faith distracter is our feelings. Our willingness to trust what God says (faith) must be placed above our emotions (feelings). One of the reasons for our anemic faith is trying to depend more on our feelings than what God says. Too often, we rely on our feelings to define the limits and extent of our obedience. If we *feel* that we are too weak, or too unworthy, then we will seek to limit the call of God in our lives. However, that is not based on fact but feeling.

Once more, we visit our friend Moses for an example when God told him to demand that Pharaoh let His people go (Exodus 4). Feeling that he did not have the status (v.1), nor the speaking ability (v.10), Moses pleaded with the Lord, "Please send someone else to do it." In response, *the Lord's anger burned against Moses* (v.11). And why wouldn't it? Moses' faithless response was saying in effect, "God, you're not to be trusted. I can't take the risk of walking into Pharaoh's palace and making such a ridiculous request. Such things are not done!" Moses violated the very point the writer of Hebrews made when he said that God must be trusted as One who rewards those who trust Him. At this point in his life, Moses did not trust God to do that. He was libeling God's character. No wonder it invoked God's angry response.

The role of feelings has always been a disruption of faith. As a good reminder, look at the description Paul gives of the acts of the sinful nature in Galatians 5:19-21. Note how many of these acts spring from "unholy emotions." Feelings have always been unstable and undependable. Isn't that why the admonitions of Scripture are based on the will and not feelings? For instance, we are never told to love one another; or to be holy; or to forgive one another; or even to tithe, if we "feel" like it. We all know where that would end! Rather, the Bible admonishes us to do it anyway—regardless of how we feel.

Ready to Begin

I remember sitting in my study one afternoon years ago when I received a call from a member of the Pastor Search Committee at Lake Norman Baptist Church where I currently serve. I listened politely as the caller described the church and asked whether or not I would be interested in a "challenge." I wasn't. As I thought about the church I was serving at that time, I reasoned, "Why should I go *there* for a challenge? I've got one *here*! I'm tired of challenges in churches. I want to go somewhere without a challenge!" It would take more to convince me that God was calling me to something new.

Famous last words because it wasn't long before I accepted God's call to serve Lake Norman Baptist. The relocation process was no different from many others' experience of serving in ministry. It began with a face-to-face conversation—putting faces with voices I'd heard on the phone and continuing forward from there. (Such is the life of a Baptist pastor!)

How different from Abraham's relocation to the land God would show him. He had no "face" to put with "The Voice" that called him. There was no preview of the challenges that lay ahead for him. He simply heard "The Voice" and responded. "The Voice" was loud enough that it shook Abraham loose from his cultural surroundings and motivated him to head off into the great unknown.

God's call to Abraham came purely by grace (Paul said as much in Romans 4:16). It was God's sovereign choice to select a single man out of a pagan and idolatrous culture. The post-Noah world had deteriorated even more than before the flood. However, it was in such a place and for such a time that God reached out by grace and called Abraham. God never lost sight of His redemptive promise given in Eden (Genesis 3:15). In Abraham, God would channel that promise through one man. There is no explanation why God chose Abraham. It was a choice sealed in mystery and grace.

Some commentators believe Abraham was approximately sixty years old when he first heard God's call. Again, what makes this call all the more special is that Abraham heard and heeded it within a culture that wasn't accustomed to hearing from God. People never heard the voice of their god, much less the voice of some unfamiliar god.

Heeding God's voice in such a disbelieving culture would have repercussions for Abraham. So it will be with us as well. As the prophet Jeremiah once said, *"But if I say, 'I will not mention him or speak any more in his name,' his word is in my heart like a fire, a fire shut up in my bones. I am weary of holding it in; indeed, I cannot"* (Jeremiah 20:9). As we'll see in the next chapter, following God's voice will alter Abraham's life. When we hear and heed God's voice, it will require re-altering our lives and re-organizing our values. When we stand at the trailhead of transforming faith, we can be sure that the life to follow will not resemble what it was before.

Trailnotes:
- Growing faith requires a willingness to follow God's voice.

- Faith is only as good as the object upon which it is placed. What is it you are trusting in? Are you trusting in God, or is your trust in "faith"?

- The need for details and our feelings can be huge distractors in faith development. Can you think of other distractions?

CHAPTER 2
Adjusting the Rearview Mirror

_"...LEAVE YOUR COUNTRY, YOUR
PEOPLE AND YOUR FATHER'S
HOUSEHOLD."(GENESIS 12:1A)_

Teaching my kids to drive was a memorable experience. First, I would very carefully instruct them to check the vital systems that would ensure their safety on the road—before starting the car. It never failed, however, that one of the first things *they* would check was the channel of the radio. I forget that for a teenager music *is* vital!

One of the areas that I tried to encourage them to check was the position of their mirrors. Of course, nothing could be further from their concern. They are not interested in what's behind. They are only interested in what's ahead (and to get there as fast and with as much rhythm as possible!).

However, what we focus on in our rearview mirror can be just as important as what we set our sights on ahead. It matters that the right things be in our rearview mirror—old habits, destructive attitudes and unhealthy relationships are just some of the things we must leave behind to follow God. Furthermore, progress requires that those things be getting smaller as we move along! What Abraham will choose to put in his rearview mirror will have a big influence on the progress he makes to the place God will show him.

Separation Matters

"Leave!" The last time God spoke this word to a human audience was in the Garden of Eden. The word described the degree of separation that was required in marriage when a *"man will leave his father and mother and be united to his wife..."* (Genesis 2:24).

Abraham's call to "leave" wasn't much different. God told him to leave something behind permanently with the idea of never returning to it again. Rightly understood, the call of faith requires a similar drastic and decisive break in our lives as well. It implies making a clean break from the influencing and controlling factors of one's past.

In order for God to use Abraham, He needed to separate him from the things that would pose a threat to their new relationship.[3] Heeding the call of God meant leaving something significant behind. God said, *"Leave your country, your people and your father's household..."* (Genesis 12:1). It would require Abraham to move from the lesser sacrifice (his country) to the greater (his father's household); the largest to the smallest; the less impactful to the most painful. That's usually how God works, isn't it? The farther you're willing to go with Him, the greater the sacrifice that is required.

Separate from Idolatry

Where Abraham began his journey, Ur of Chaldea, was a pleasant place. There is a modern view among some commentators that it was located near the Persian Gulf. Thousands of years of silt deposits from the great Tigris and Euphrates Rivers have pushed Ur back approximately 100 miles inland from its original, ancient location near the Gulf. It was a land of rich soil and abundant crops. The idea of leaving such an oasis to journey across the burning Arabian Desert to an unknown place seemed totally unreasonable. And it was. Oh, and by the way, Ur was also noted for something else—idolatry.

I live in a beautiful community in North Carolina

---

3   Note how God was *always* trying to separate Abraham from other things. Sometimes these things took the form of places (*e.g.,* Ur or Haran or Egypt). Sometimes it was material things (*e.g.,* the recovered goods of Genesis 14:21ff). Sometimes it was people (*e.g.,* Hagar, Lot and eventually even his treasured son Isaac).

that lies adjacent to Lake Norman. (It's a tough gig, but somebody's got to do it!) It is a vibrant and growing community with many professional and recreational opportunities. It is also a very prosperous community. Many white- collar professionals and even sporting professionals call this community home. However, like Ur, it is a community steeped in idolatry. Recreation, leisure and materialism are just some of the gods that rule the mindset of this community. Idolatry is not something relegated to ancient civilizations. Idolatry is alive and well in my community...and I bet it is in yours as well.

Nevertheless, we rarely recognize idolatry when we see it. One of my best friends is Greg Mathis, the Senior Pastor of a great church in western North Carolina. Two elderly ladies that attend his church were overheard talking one day at a local spa. One of the ladies said, "I just don't understand the problem that Pastor Mathis has with Dollar Tree. I think it is a fine store. I've shopped there for years and I like it! But Pastor Mathis was putting this store down in his sermon Sunday." The other lady replied, "Honey, he wasn't talking about Dollar Tree. He was talking about I-DOL-A-TRY!" We hear what we want to hear, I suppose.

We've lost a true sense of what idolatry really is. Gone are the idols of wood, stone or elements of nature. Our contemporary idols are much more sophisticated and "civilized." Our idols are made of chrome and fiberglass, stucco and mortar, and they come "with a fabulous view." Other idols are more intangible. They take the form of power, prestige, promotions and peer pressure.

Idols—ancient or modern—all have the same power to command and control us. They command our allegiance every waking hour. They control our thinking and life perspective. We bow down to these sources of status and self-esteem and pay homage to them. They control us and we give ourselves over to their sway. We not only heed their every command but also let them define us as well.

The call to Abraham to leave his country was no small matter. There would be more sacrifices to come and more things he'd have to leave. However, this is where it began with Abraham: the call to follow a new Voice. The trail for us begins here as well. God must be God. He will accept nothing less.

Separate from Comfort

A second area of separation required from Abraham was in the area of "his family." It was an uncomfortable request. Leaving his clan meant leaving a comfortable environment. This was the place where he was raised. His clan represented the collective conscience that had instilled in him his sense of values. Abraham felt comfortable there. Ur was safe.

It's always comfortable and safe where you march lockstep in line according to the expectations of others. Comfortable, yes, but also limiting. Tucked safely within the limits of Ur, Abraham would never see his full potential. Safe within his clan, he wouldn't have to think. He wouldn't have to wrestle with competing values. In Ur, there was no such competition. Everything was the same. Up until he heard God's voice, Abraham was safely within his cocoon. He was told what to believe and how to behave. But to leave all this, Abraham would have to redefine his worldview. He would now be following another compass, another life perspective—all determined by this new Voice he heard.

The voice of God that speaks to us beckons us to follow another set of values—ones shaped by the principles of God. His values are to be the influencing principles upon which our belief and subsequent behavior rest.

Let's be honest. It's extremely uncomfortable to step outside the accepted values of our community. To reject the sources that have once influenced us is extremely difficult…and often dangerous. No wonder Jesus warned in Matthew 10:24-25, *"A student is not above his teacher, nor a servant above his master…If the head of the house has been called Beelzebub, how much more the members of his household!"*

Separate from Safety

The call to separate from one's father and household was risky in ancient times. It meant turning one's back on one of the few safety nets available. Family was the only "social security" to protect you when you got sick, injured or old. Moving away was a scary thought when there was nothing else to fall back on. As Abraham said his good-byes to idolatry, comfort and safety, this last sacrifice was by far the hardest.

Abraham's call to leave his father's household reminds us of a danger we face in the pursuit of God. The pull and influence of family—those closest to us—often pose the greatest threat to our response to God's voice. As head of the clan, his father Terah would have been a rival influence on Abraham's allegiance. (Remember, they were pagans—no one had even heard of God!) Terah was still calling the shots in Abraham's life at this point because of cultural expectations.

In similar fashion, our families may rise up and protest the loudest when we alter our lifestyle for "spiritual reasons." When we start following God to such a degree that we are acting out of character to our families, their well-meaning protests will be heard above all other voices. Over the centuries, these protests have been issued in various ways:

- "Look, it's okay to go to church and be a Christian if you want. But why go overseas and do missionary work there? Aren't there plenty of people you could help around here?"
- "Why go into full-time ministry? Your dad and I had hoped you would take over the family business. Your grandfather started it, you know."
- "You've joined *what* church? But you were already baptized as a baby!"

Jesus warned about this family pull. He said, *"If anyone comes to me and does not hate his father and mother, his wife and children, his brothers and sisters—yes, even his own life—he cannot be my disciple. And anyone who does not carry his cross and follow me cannot be my disciple"* (Luke 14:26).

Why would Jesus make such a requirement? He knew that family responsibilities would sometimes present distractions that could challenge deeper discipleship. Jesus knew that transforming faith doesn't come without serious commitment. A devout follower of Christ must turn from anything that poses a distraction from hearing and following God. Sometimes good things can keep us from doing the best things.

However, we serve a God that *"rewards"* our steps of faith (Hebrews 11:6). The blessings God promised would more than replace everything Abraham would give up to follow Him (Genesis 12:2-3). Abraham would leave his country, but God promised to make him into *"a great nation."* Abraham would leave his people, but God promised to make his name *"great"* among all people of the earth. Abraham would be forced to leave his father's household to pursue the higher calling of God, but God repeatedly promised blessings as a reward not only to him but also to *"all peoples on earth."*

Jesus offered the same assurance to the disciples who followed Him. *"Peter said to him, 'We have left all we had to follow you!' 'I tell you the truth,' Jesus said to them, 'no one who has left home or wife or brothers or parents or children for the sake of the kingdom of God will fail to receive many times as much in this age and, in the age to come, eternal life'"* (Luke 18:28-29).

Is there any area of your life where you are holding on to something (or someone) that poses a rival to God's development of your spiritual life? What have you hesitated to give up, thinking the cost is too high? Beware of anything that you refuse to leave—anything that keeps pulling you away from fulfilling the calling of God. Don't stay in Ur. A new land beckons. However, to get there, you must be willing to position your life so that you have the right things in your rearview mirror as you move forward in faith. Whatever limits your full potential for God must be decreasing in size in your rearview mirror if you are making progress down this new path of transforming faith.

Never the Same
Oliver Wendell Holmes once said, "The mind is like a rubber band. Once stretched, it never returns to its original size." In the next chapter, Abraham finds out how true that is in one's spiritual journey as well. A lot of stretching will take place between Ur and the unknown land ahead.

Abraham is about to be stretched, even contorted, through a series of tests that will challenge every spiritual fiber of his being. He will be bruised and battered while making his way down the trail of faith. The person Abraham was in Ur we will hardly recognize later atop Mt. Moriah. Likewise, the call of God stretches you in ways that you can't imagine until you can no longer remain the same.

Trailnotes

- Progressing down the trail of faith requires that we leave some things behind. What are some of the things that you have had to put in your "rearview mirror" in order to grow in your faith?

- Idolatry comes in many forms. What are the "gods" that you have had to forsake?

- Whatever sacrifices we make as an investment in our intimacy with God, God will abundantly replace.

CHAPTER 3

A "Sorry" Start

"SO ABRAM LEFT, AS THE LORD HAD TOLD HIM; AND LOT WENT WITH HIM. ABRAM WAS SEVENTY-FIVE YEARS OLD WHEN HE SET OUT FROM HARAN."
(GENESIS 12:5)

Basketball is a fast-paced, up-and-down-the-court game where one team tries to outscore the other. For all the changes that have evolved in basketball since its inventor James Naismith put two peach baskets on the railing inside a gym, the game is still fundamentally the same. Because the object is to "out-score" one's opponent, scoring has become the most celebrated part of the game. Let's face it—it's not often that ESPN will include highlights of rebounds. Scoring is king!

However, for all its attention, scoring is only a *part* of the game. Actually, a small part. Rebounding is important because of missed shots. No team—or player—is so good that they make all their shots. Rarely do they even make half! It is what a team does *after* a shot is taken (and missed) that often determines whether they will win or lose.

Michael Jordan is believed by many to be the best basketball player who ever played the game. His accomplishments on the court are well chronicled. Jordan played 13 seasons for the Chicago Bulls of the NBA, while averaging over 30 points per game. During his career, the Bulls won six championships. No one would question Jordan's greatness in the game of basketball.

You don't become great by being one-dimensional, of course. Even though he is most noted for his scoring, Jordan was great in all aspects of the game. An interesting statistic of Jordan's career, however, is that he only made .497% of his shots. In this area alone, Jordan was technically more of a failure than a success. For every shot he made, he also missed one. Fortunately for him, Jordan had teammates that specialized in "failure." One such player you may remember was Dennis Rodman. For all his colorful antics on and off the court, Rodman was a superior rebounder, with a career average of over 23 rebounds per game. Rodman made a name for himself by capitalizing on other's mistakes. Without him, it could be argued that the Bulls would never have won all those championships.

The trail of transforming faith is often beset with disappointment and mistakes. As Jean La Fontaine once wrote, "...*there is no road of flowers leading to glory.*"[4] Many bumps and bruises will shape this trail of faith that Abraham now travels. Abraham is a long way from the finished product of Moriah. He reminds me of the story of the doctor who came home from a long day at the hospital. His wife asked him how his day went. The doctor said, "*Not too good. I had a patient who drank a quart of varnish.*" His wife responded, "*Oh no. Well, I guess that was the end of him.*" "*Yes,*" the doctor replied, "*but it sure was a glossy finish!*" Abraham was far from the polish and gloss of a Moriah faith. There would be many "missed shots" and rebounds along the way.

"Sorrreeee!"

Have you ever played the board game "Sorry"? Players start out by rolling dice and moving the number of spaces rolled. Sounds simple doesn't it? But it's more involved than that. Sometimes you land on a space that advances you even further. (That's the fun part—to advance, move forward and progress.) Sometimes you even land in someone else's space—that's even more fun because you get to send him or her all the way back to the start. My wife has this heinous and diabolical way of yelling "Sorrreeee!" when this happens to me. (While I've never

---

4   Jean de La Fontaine, *Fables, The Merriam-Webster Dictionary of Quotations*, Merriam-Webster, Inc., 1992, p.167.

doubted my salvation, playing "Sorry" with her has made me doubt hers.) Sometimes you land on a different space that makes you take several steps back. I hate the backward steps.

The trail of transforming faith is a lot like the game of Sorry. It would become for Abraham a familiar game, and he would learn to play it well. Like many of us, he would take a step forward in his faith and seem to make progress, only to take a step backward soon after. For example, when he originally left for Canaan (11:31a), we see that he takes a major step of faith forward. However, he stops short of the destination, choosing to settle in Haran instead with his father (11:31b). After a while there, we see Abraham take another step forward when he obeyed God's call and resumes his journey to Canaan again (12:4a). And yet taking Lot with him (12:4b) is a wrong move, and it eventually sets him back another step. Thankfully, finally Abraham takes a series of steps forward by building altars and worshipping God (12:7, 8). Let's take a closer look at each one of these steps—forward and backward—in Abraham's journey.

One Step Forward—Departing from Ur

Terah took his son Abram, his grandson Lot son of Haran, and his daughter-in-law Sarai, the wife of his son Abram, and together they set out from Ur of the Chaldeans to go to Canaan.[5] (Genesis 11:31a)

---

5   You will notice the names "Abram" and "Sarai" used here. Actually, the name "Abraham" did not come until much later (17:5) when God would change his name from "father of many" (Abram) to "father of a multitude" (Abraham). God would also change Sarai's name to "Sarah." For the sake of familiarity and consistency, I am using the later forms of both names throughout this book, unless quoting directly from Scripture.

I've often wondered what it must have been like for Abraham as he started out from Ur. What kind of person must he have been to willingly break from the comfortable surroundings of Ur and journey to a place not yet known? The writer of Genesis 11:31 seems to shield Abraham from that initial decision because we get the idea that Abraham was more of a follower than a leader regarding this departure. Perhaps due to the proper cultural protocol of the time, Terah (Abraham's father) gets top billing. However, Acts 7:2 gives use more insight into this move away from Ur because we see that the break from Ur was actually Abraham's idea. It was *his* calling. It would be *his* faith that would be on the line.

In making his bold step from Ur, Abraham reminds us that the will of God is not always certain when we first embark upon it. Abraham didn't know, and neither do we, where the road ahead might lead. Like a hiker along a foliage-covered trail where only an occasional clearing brings a glimpse of the summit into view, Abraham's journey will be shrouded with uncertainty. He will have to get used to this uncertainty. Abraham will learn that God can, and will be, specific when He needs to be. However, there are many times when He doesn't need to be specific. In those times, God will simply say, "Go." Such times will require that we trust Him to be specific when it becomes necessary for God to do so. By going, Abraham takes one positive step forward—hooray for Abraham!

One Step Back—Settling in Haran
But when they came to Haran, they settled there. (Genesis 11:31b)

No sooner had Abraham taken his first step forward than he makes a strategic mistake. It was unintentional, but it would prove to be a disruption of his faith nonetheless and result in one step backward in faith.

A closer examination of the passage in Acts 7 points out an interesting omission. It seems that while in Ur, Abraham was never told to leave his "father's household." That bit of information only came to him when he was in Haran some 15 years later. He was only told in Ur, *"Leave your country and your people..."* (Acts 7:3). No mention is given of leaving his father's household. When he started out from Ur, there is no reason to believe that he was compromising God's call by taking with him his father and various other relatives. However, taking along these extra family members would later prove to be a mistake.

Like Abraham, sometimes we mean well, but it just doesn't turn out the way we intend. We start out with a sincere willingness to follow God wherever He leads. But whether it is a lack of information or lack of experience, we convince ourselves that we can handle the accessories that we try to include in our journey—things that in hindsight we know should have been left behind.

What we think are minor things can turn out to be really big problems. Sometimes we do err in sincerity, but sincere error can lead to failure just the same. But we can't fault Abraham too severely for being new at this game of faith. You can bet that the lessons learned here will be applied later.

The added accessories (family members) that he brought along would prove to be disruptive. In fact, Abraham would stop far short of God's intended desire for him. Such is the pull of family.

Having traveled many miles with a wife and

three kids, I can only imagine how many times Abraham must have heard after leaving Ur, *"How much longer is it?" "I've got to go to the bathroom!" "He is bothering me!"* I wonder if Abraham had to divide up the backseat like I did on occasion and "dare anyone to cross that line"! My wife had an interesting motivator that she would include on trips called a fly swatter. Such a tool was useful not only to eliminate pesky flies (which, by the way, were rarely found in our car!) but also to keep arms and hands from venturing over the "no swat zone." Once while trying to make her point in the backseat, she actually clipped my right ear!

I don't know if Sarah ever used such a motivator or not, but for whatever reason, when Abraham came to Haran, he decided that he had had enough. Haran would serve as a rest stop. But it would be a stop that would last for 15 years.

You can lose a lot of faith in 15 years. You can even begin to think that the rest stop is your actual place of destination. I've never vacationed at a rest stop, but I have on occasion been tempted to leave kids there. Admittedly, I have "pulled over" at various times in my spiritual journey. Having grown weary of all the "backseat drama," I've stopped my progress temporarily. Have you ever done that? Abraham did. He pulled over and stopped at a rest stop so long that his father died.

I've never seen a grave at a rest stop before. (I have been tempted to create some, however.) After burying his father there, Abraham discovers that God is lessening his load for him. No longer stalled in his faith, Abraham would now venture forward again—this time a little lighter.

Another Step Forward—Leaving Haran

The LORD had said to Abram, "Leave your country, your people and your father's household and go to the land I will show you…" So Abram left, as the LORD had told him. (Genesis 12:1, 4a)

It is by the grace of God that we are ever called in the first place. However, once heard and brushed aside, there is no reason to think that God is ever obligated to repeat that call again. The fact that God *does* repeat that original call to us is truly a testimony of God's tireless effort in grace. In Genesis 12:1ff, God once again extends His grace to Abraham. Thank God for his second (and third, and fourth and even beyond!) call. After 15 years of silence at the rest stop in Haran, now the call comes again to Abraham. What must Abraham have thought during those fifteen silent years? Had he wondered if he had forever blown his chance by not continuing with his journey? Did he think God had even changed His mind, and the call heard in Ur had now expired?

How wonderful to be given a second chance! The call of Abraham in Genesis 12 seemed to be exactly that—a second chance. Given another opportunity to prove his faithfulness, Abraham would not stop until he would arrive at the place called simply "the land."

As I think about this second call, I can't help to be reminded of an unpleasant, but real truth. Terah, Abraham's father, is now gone. He died in Haran (Genesis 11:32). For all the good he may have once been, Terah seems now to have been nothing more than a hindrance to Abraham in pursuing his obedience to God. We have no way of knowing for sure, but it's likely that Terah refused to let Abraham go as directed earlier. Terah may have decided to go with him simply because he may have been unwilling to give up his control over Abraham. As his elder, it is likely that Terah was still calling the shots in Abraham's life. For all of his good intents and purposes, Terah may have been responsible for stopping Abraham short of God's promised blessing.

Yet now Terah is now gone. God has a way of removing our excuses for half-hearted obedience. How many times has God had to remove the "Terahs" from your life? (Or, a more disturbing thought: Could you actually be playing the role of Terah in someone else's faith journey?) How many times has God had to pry out of our hands the crutches that we allowed to keep us from total submission to His will? Terahs died hard. But every trail of transforming faith must be littered with these "Terah graves" along the way.

What is buried in your "Terah" grave? Maybe your Terah was the other "voice" that you gave allegiance to that God would not share. Maybe Terah was the reason you could not give God your whole-hearted obedience. Regardless of what it may be, your Terah must also "die' before moving along the trail of faith. Leaving Terah would prepare Abraham for another, more painful separation later...Isaac. But for now, funeral over, Terah gone...Abraham soon makes another step.

Another Step Back—A "Lot" of Trouble
...and Lot went with him. (Genesis 12:4a)

Uh oh—this can't be good! Well, that certainly didn't take long. It was hard for Abraham to create any momentum on his new trail of faith because it seems he kept shooting himself in the foot. It would not be so evident now, but Lot would turn out to be big trouble later. He was a family member that Abraham should have left behind, but he took him along instead. There was a reason God told Abraham to "*leave your…father's household*." Lot was some of the baggage Abraham should have left in Haran. In fact, Abraham had a "Lot" of baggage. (Sorry, I couldn't resist.)

What are some of the old bags that we continue to carry in our faith journey? (I could make a joke here, but my wife may read this.) Seriously now, the baggage we carry on our faith journey has a way of impacting the journey for us and for others around us. If you've ever flown with a stubborn passenger who just could not bring himself to check his baggage *before* the flight, you know something of which I speak. He comes rolling down the aisle with a bag that Fed Ex would find challenging. Then he tries to squeeze that "camel into the eye of a needle" (also called the overhead compartment). Your excess baggage doesn't just impact your journey, but it has a way of making others uncomfortable as well.

What are some of the "bags" that we refuse to check-in before the journey? Maybe it is that self-doubt that convinces you that you simply don't measure up. Or, maybe it is the painful embarrassment of a humiliating failure. Or, maybe it is just a dumb reaction to something that still haunts us.

Whatever it is, may I suggest a simple solution? Just check it. Come clean with God; tell Him all about it. (You might as well, for He already knows anyway!) Leave it at the counter, and let Him handle it. Travel light. Those pesky hidden baggage fees have been around for a long time. Just ask Abraham. The cost of his baggage would be expensive, and it would result in one step back.

Another Step Forward—Arriving in Canaan!

Abram was seventy-five years old when he set out from Haran. He took his wife Sarai, his nephew Lot, all the possessions they had accumulated and the people they had acquired in Haran, and they set out for the land of Canaan, and they arrived there.

Abram traveled through the land as far as the site of the great tree of Moreh at Shechem. At that time the Canaanites were in the land. The LORD appeared to Abram and said, "To your offspring I will give this land." So he built an altar there to the LORD, who had appeared to him. (Genesis 12:4b-7)

Having packed up all that he and Sarah possessed into the family caravan, once again they are off to Canaan. Hebrews 11:10 tells us that *"he was looking forward to the city with foundations, whose architect and builder is God."* Abraham was energized by the vision of a spiritual place in the midst of physical reality. Such visions still propel us forward in faith.

When Abraham and his crew *"arrived there"* (v.5), it was a special moment. The land that had seemed so impossible just a short time earlier was now reality. Good work, Abraham! Arriving in Canaan is even more impressive considering that this might not have happened had Abraham made some of the excuses that often derail us. For example, the passage indicates that Abraham had many possessions. Plus, he was no spring chicken (the Bible says he was seventy-five years old). And what about that fresh memory of 15 lost years in Haran?

Like Abraham, sometimes I hear people complain that they just are "too busy" with too many responsibilities to follow God's call. Or, they claim they are too old to learn "Canaanese," or they don't have all the education they think they need, or they have made too many mistakes before. To his credit, Abraham could have tried to disqualify himself with similar excuses. But the vision and the Voice were too strong.

Yet Another Step Forward—Focusing on Worship

Abraham was content to live in a tent as a traveling pilgrim in a strange land, but he took the time to build an altar to the Lord (12:7). Unconcerned with his own physical comfort, he is more concerned that God is comfortable with him. Upon arriving in Canaan, he makes two discoveries. First, he finds out that wicked and pagan inhabitants—Canaanites—already occupy the land. Fortunately, he makes another discovery: God was there, too. The same God that spoke to him in Ur and Haran was also in this strange and uncertain place called Canaan. Isn't it reassuring to know that whatever your strange and uncertain situation, God is already there? In full assurance, Abraham built an altar and worshipped God. This consecrated action would become a significant part of Abraham's faith journey. In that quiet moment of worshipful surrender, Abraham would be reminded of how frail he was to meet the challenges of the Canaanites and how shallow were the things he held in his possession.

Like him, we need those "altars" in our own life journeys. We need to meet God every day in worshipful surrender and there seek the strength to face the "Canaanites" challenging us. It is in such times and in such a place that God discloses Himself to us. We cannot progress on the trail of transformation without personal times of worship. Whenever we build such an altar, it is a step in the right direction.

Genesis 12:8 marks the second time we are told that Abraham built an altar to worship God. "*From there he went on toward the hills east of Bethel and pitched his tent, with Bethel on the west and Ai on the east. There he built an altar to the LORD and called on the name of the LORD.*" Finally, we start to see some progress and meaningful movement toward "Moriah." Though still a long way off, the spiritual strength to face the ultimate test of Moriah is closer now. Worship is being engraved into the fabric of his life. He is growing spiritually. This is a good thing. One of the measures of growth is captured in the phrase: "*...there he built an altar to the Lord and called on the name of the Lord.*"

Living a nomadic lifestyle, there seems to be no attempt to make a name for himself. Instead, he was quite willing to "*call on the name of the Lord.*" What seemed to matter most to Abraham wasn't his own name but the Lord's. The irony here is that by choosing such a selfless way, Abraham would become a name for all generations to follow. Jesus would later say, "*For whoever wants to save his life will lose it, but whoever loses his life for me...will save it*" (Mark 8:35).

Abraham reminds us that following the Lord will bring its own rewards. We are often too blinded to see the true picture of how God rewards us, however. Let me illustrate. Did you know that Abraham had a brother named Nahor? While some of you may know this story well enough to recall that bit of trivia, let's look at it from another direction. The Bible tells us that Nahor built a city and named it after himself (Genesis 24:10). (I've always wondered what it would be like to live in "Blantonsville." Hmm, has a nice ring to it.) I'm sure if you were to go to the city of Nahor and ask its citizens to identify the most successful of Terah's boys...Abraham or Nahor...their first response would be, "Who is Abraham? Abraham we don't know. We heard about him once, but what a problem child he must have been. We heard he was a restless one and moved far away to Canaan. But Nahor, well, he's the successful one! He's the founder of our town!"

It never would have occurred to the Nahorites then that the great founding father of their town would go down in history without the same name recognition of his brother Abraham. Don't judge success (or failure!) too quickly. What we may judge today as one thing may in fact turn out to be quite the contrary later. God has His timing and His rewards. That's the course that Abraham chose. It didn't seem at the time to be the most successful route, but time would prove otherwise. Congratulations, Abraham! You're making progress.

However, as we'll see in the next few chapters, a series of tests loomed on the horizon—ones that would strike fear in his heart, sift his character and bring many doubts. His first test was immediate and intense. In the next chapter, we'll find out how Abraham managed this initial test and we'll explore the life lessons he learned.

Trailnotes:

- The trail of faith is often beset with many failures. Don't get discouraged!

- The pull and influence of family can sometimes challenge our response to God's call.

- Sadly, God sometimes has to remove our "Terahs" before we can make progress in our faith journey. What "Terahs" has God had to remove from your life?

- Upon his arrival in Canaan, Abraham discovered God was already there! Wherever God calls you, He is already there waiting for you.

- Don't judge success (or failure) too quickly. It might not be what you initially think.

CHAPTER 4

The Test of Confidence

¹⁰ *Now there was a famine in the land, and Abram went down to Egypt to live there for a while because the famine was severe.* ¹¹ *As he was about to enter Egypt, he said to his wife Sarai, "I know what a beautiful woman you are.* ¹² *When the Egyptians see you, they will say, 'This is his wife.' Then they will kill me but will let you live.* ¹³ *Say you are my sister, so that I will be treated well for your sake and my life will be spared because of you."*

¹⁴ *When Abram came to Egypt, the Egyptians saw*

that she was a very beautiful woman. ¹⁵ *And when Pharaoh's officials saw her, they praised her to Pharaoh, and she was taken into his palace.* ¹⁶ *He treated Abram well for her sake, and Abram acquired sheep and cattle, male and female donkeys, menservants and maidservants, and camels.*

¹⁷ *But the* LORD *inflicted serious diseases on Pharaoh and his household because of Abram's wife Sarai.* ¹⁸ *So Pharaoh summoned Abram. "What have you done to me?" he said. "Why didn't you tell me she was your wife?* ¹⁹ *Why did you say, 'She is my sister,' so that I took her to be my wife? Now then, here is your wife. Take her and go!"* ²⁰ *Then Pharaoh gave orders about Abram to his men, and they sent him on his way, with his wife and everything he had.* (Genesis 12:10-20)

When I grew up, we didn't seem to be as afraid of things as we are today. We didn't have those bulky bike helmets or skateboard padding. Kids today look like rolling armadillos. In my day, you suffered head injuries and dealt with it! We had no child restraint system or air bags. We had Mama's right arm! Those were the days.

Probably in no other time in our nation's history have so many been so fearful about so much. Someone has said regarding our paranoia, "We can eat bland food so we don't get ulcers; drink only bottled water; go to bed early; avoid the night life and red meat; mind our own business and never get in arguments; save all the money we can… and then slip in the bathtub and break our neck." Fear is the reward of sin—part of the fallen human condition. No wonder Jesus described the last days as a time when men's hearts would be failing them because of fear (Luke 21:26).

Fear erodes our confidence in God, and it became an issue that Abraham would have to face squarely as he traveled down the next mile on the trail of transforming faith.

What's It Gonna Be...Fear or Faith?

I'm a pretty coordinated person. I can rub my stomach and pat my head at the same time. Impressed? But there are some things I've found that I can't do...like exercise both fear and faith at the same time. Neither can you. Fear and faith are like the opposite ends of a seesaw. When one is up, the other is down. They are polar opposites and one tends to offset the other. When your faith is strong, your fear is weak. Unfortunately for Abraham, we are about to see him seated fairly high on the "fear end" of that seesaw. We have an advantage over Abraham in that we know where he will eventually end up...at Moriah. Moriah will be a place of faith, captured in the confidence behind Abraham's words, *"God will provide"* (Genesis 22:8). But before he arrives at that Moriah moment, there is much to do in his faith development. From where he sits now, Abraham doesn't seem to have that level of confidence. Afraid that God wouldn't provide during an intense famine, he's about to turn south toward Egypt. It would be another test that God would use to develop Abraham into a useful servant. How was God able to take a raw, undeveloped follower from a culture of idol worship and develop him into a mighty man of Moriah faith? Where would this Moriah confidence come from? How would it be developed?

I find it difficult to define faith apart from the idea of confidence. God develops our confidence in him in several different ways, which we see illustrated in the life of Abraham. First, Abraham faced a difficult circumstance.

Facing Difficult Circumstances

I once had a conversation with a member of our church who happened to be sitting at the traffic light, waiting for a green light to make a left turn onto a bridge in Minneapolis, Minnesota. The date was August 1, 2007, and the bridge was the now infamous I-35 West Bridge. Suddenly, this person heard a rumbling and the bridge collapsed, plunging approximately 100 vehicles into the water 115 feet below. The collapse resulted in 13 fatalities and 145 injuries. Reports would later reveal that the bridge had been inspected prior to the collapse and was found to be "structurally deficient" on at least two separate occasions.

The science of bridge construction far exceeds my comprehension. Admittedly, I know nothing about civil engineering and what goes into making such structures strong and reliable. I do know, however, that bridges are supposed to be inspected for stress by using stress. By subjecting a structure to stressful conditions, engineers gain confidence that it will perform as needed.

This principle far exceeds testing bridges because our own confidence is developed under stressful conditions. Under duress, we get a true picture of our confidence in our heavenly Father. When we last left Abraham in a previous chapter, he was building altars. Worship had become a meaningful part of his relationship with God. Now the worth of that worship will be tested in crisis. Likewise, sometimes our most intense and satisfying moments in worship are followed by some of the most gut-wrenching, faith-challenging circumstances we'll ever face. It was no less true for Jesus' disciples. Their transfiguring moment of worship on the mountaintop with Christ where they saw His glory was followed by a crisis in the valley below with a demon the disciples could not cast out (Luke 9:37-40). Having just witnessed an inexpressible vision of Christ in the third heaven, Paul says that he was given a *"thorn in the flesh"* so that he would know the sufficiency of the Lord's grace (2 Corinthians 12:2-9). It is those "thorny" moments of crisis that test the worth and object of our worship.

Problems, setbacks, economic downturns and other trying circumstances seem to contradict our view of God's goodness (and justice!), and they challenge our confidence in God. Soon after Abraham received God's promise of blessing, a famine hits. Famines don't usually fit our idea of blessing! Besides, famines seem so unfair. Like Abraham, we rarely see God's wider purpose. "Famines" are allowed entry into our lives for a very specific purpose—to strengthen our faith. God does nothing through us apart from our faith. It was through famine that his faith would flourish. Abraham would have to learn to trust not in the circumstances, but in the provision of God. He needed to learn that God could provide, even in the midst of adverse circumstances. This is a challenge for disciples of all ages.

Abraham's famine is really no different from the disciple Peter's embarrassing moment in the storm when he asked the Lord's permission to walk across the water and come to Him (Matthew 14:22-33). Permission granted, now what? He ended up sinking, but at least he got out of the boat! He was willing to do something no one else in the boat was willing to do (or for that matter, had ever done before!). I love that about Peter. That was a defining moment for him, and Peter would learn a hard lesson when he realized that the Lord must be held within our confidence in order for Him to use us to do great things. Our buoyancy upon the stormy seas of life is not based on our own skills, but it rests solely upon the Lord.

Uncomfortable though it is for us, He will allow us at times to sink in order to refocus our confidence. It never ceases to amaze me when I ask someone, "How are you doing?" and they reply, "Under the circumstances, okay." I can't help but smile. I think back upon Peter's "sinking spell" and say to myself, "If that were true of Peter, he would have drowned!"

Under the circumstances is not a place to be. Abraham (and Peter) remind us that being under the circumstances can be a costly place to be. Don't allow your circumstances to determine your confidence.

The Fallout of Bad Choices

Every choice comes with consequences. There are no exceptions to this rule. One of the ways God develops our confidence in Him is by allowing us to lose confidence in ourselves. We can learn some valuable lessons from Abraham regarding bad choices.

A bad choice usually comes from a quick decision.

Bad things tend to happen when we move quickly. There are exceptions to this rule, of course. However, immediately after the famine hit Abraham's world, he took quick action and headed south. Being a proud Southerner myself, I can certainly understand his desire to go south. But according to a map of Canaan, south is toward Egypt. It's hard to imagine that Egypt would have offered Abraham any real benefit. (That would be like me heading from North Carolina to Georgia!) Be careful about making quick, hasty decisions under pressure. We are all eternally grateful for a carpenter named Joseph whose story reminds us to slow down and consider our options. Having discovered his beloved Mary was expecting a baby, had he made a quick and hasty decision he could have divorced her—even had her stoned! Think about the eternal repercussions of that! Yet the Bible says, *"After he had considered this, an angel of the Lord appeared."* Give God a chance to show up—what's the hurry?

A bad choice is sometimes the most reasonable of our choices.

I tread lightly here for I am perfectly aware that God gives us a brain for a very specific purpose…to use! Nevertheless, God doesn't always prefer the reasonable choice. There are many examples in the Bible where God asked His servants to do something that seemed so illogical and unreasonable. Noah is a ready example. The subject of rain had never been mentioned in the Bible before Noah was told to build an ark in preparation for a flood. This plan certainly didn't endear Noah to his neighbors. I imagine Noah got a lot of nasty notices from his homeowners association!

Likewise, the decision to go to Egypt may have been a "reasonable" one given the situation, but whose "reason"? Ironically, had Abraham inquired of God, He may have sent him to Egypt anyway. I know I just said some bad things about Egypt (and Georgia). For that, I apologize…to Egypt. But allow me to humble myself and admit one very real possibility. There are several examples in the Bible of God sending His servants to Egypt for a specific purpose. Jacob will later descend south with his sons during another famine, and that was certainly within God's approval. Mary and Joseph, again under God's direction, would flee Herod's murderous intent to Egypt. So it is entirely possible that God would have sent him there anyway. However, Abraham went there following his *own* wisdom—not God's. Sometimes you do the right thing, but you can do it the wrong way and at the wrong time and God will not bless it. Why? The reason for this is the issue of God's glory.

Abraham's sin was that he failed to give God the glory! The idea of glory is having one's unique attributes put on clear and open display. Literally, it means to shine the spotlight upon someone, bringing out his or her wonderful abilities and skills. The Bible says that we were created to glorify God. Throughout all of our lives and in all of our circumstances, God places us in opportunities that put Him in the best possible light. These situations may seem uncomfortable for us, but it's not about us. *It is about Him.* The "famines" we face give God the opportunity to demonstrate to the world (and to us!) that He is the all-sufficient and sustaining God. This is what Abraham robbed from God. Abraham turned off the spotlight and prevented God's splendor to shine through him.

A bad choice comes in the absence of worship.
We saw previously how Abraham built an altar to worship when he stopped along the path to Canaan. When the Bible says, "Abraham left Bethel—the place of worship," these words are rich in symbolism. In Egypt, he is away from his altars of worship. No such mention of altars or worship in Egypt. Abraham, it seems, traded one kind of famine for another—a famine of worshiping the true God.

There was a logical sequence to what Abraham was experiencing. He made a reasonable decision in his wisdom because he stopped trusting God. Abraham had painted himself into a corner. Our actions always trend toward the source of our confidence—God or ourselves.

Young people sometimes go off to college with strong faith but soon fall into moral sin. They stop reading the Bible, praying and worshipping—what happened? While their profession of faith was once up, their practice of that same faith is now down. They can't endure the inconsistency for long, but they are not willing to give up whatever sin brought their practice down. So, they do the only thing a guilty conscious will allow them to do. They lower their profession to match the level of practice. They begin to discount Christianity as "just a bunch of hypocrites." Or they say, "I don't have to go to church with self-righteous people." Our actions always reflect the source of our confidence, or lack of it.

Sin will keep you from effective, meaningful worship. It is just as true, however, that meaningful worship will keep you from sin. In fact worship is a "litmus" test of the vitality of your personal walk with God. Is worship a chore for you? Do you come to worship with a sense of duty? Do you spend your time looking at your watch or thinking about where you are going for lunch afterwards? Can you hardly wait to get home? If that's true, then maybe somewhere in your immediate past you made a bad choice to stop trusting God and it's ruining your worship.

The Failure of Flawed Character

Our confidence in what God *can* do is more clearly evident when we contrast it against the backdrop of what we *can't* do. We are, as the Bible clearly says, sinners— none righteous, no, not a single one of us. Abraham got a good taste of that reality when he went to Egypt and was tempted to concoct a story based on lies because he was afraid of the Pharaoh. Abraham got to see what was inside of him. When squeezed by the pressures of this life, what's inside of us (our character) will come out.

Abraham now finds himself on the horns of a dilemma. First, he decides to abandon his faith and flee to the greener grass of Egypt. But in doing so, he removes himself from the umbrella of God's protection. Robbing God of His glory, Abraham was now calling the shots in his own life and assuming responsibility for the outcome. Unfortunately, he has now created another situation where he fears for his safety among the Egyptians because of Sarah's beauty and the attention she would attract among the Egyptians. He was afraid they would kill him in order to take Sarah. Hey, here's a question for you Abraham: *"Did you not think of that before ever deciding to leave Canaan?"*

Like Abraham, we often create dilemmas for ourselves. Leaving God's will removes us from His protection and requires that we assume the responsibility for the outcome. I often hear the complaint among those who are suffering as a result of disobedience, *"God, how could you? Why are you doing this to me?"* It rarely occurs to them that they now have to experience the consequences of a poor choice. Somewhere in our past, we decided to leave our life of faith and trek out on our own, call our own shots, be our own person, follow our own rules. However, when we find ourselves in troubling circumstances of our own creation, we cry out to God as one mistreated.

Making the first decision to leave God is sometimes the most difficult. But having made that choice, other poor choices seem to come much easier. One bad decision seems to be quickly followed by another. Once we turn our eyes away from God, we are easily influenced by the values and schemes that govern the new land where we now hope to be accepted. Egypt, Abraham discovers, has its own challenges. To fit comfortably within Egypt, he will have to do as the Egyptians do, quite aware that he faces danger as an "outsider." He fears that Pharaoh will kill him and he somehow convinces Sarah that it will be her fault if that happens! (People in the grip of sin rarely see the trouble as being of their own making. It's usually someone else's fault.) Even at age sixty-five, Sarah must have possessed all of the physical allure of a very beautiful woman many years younger. We're talking some serious Oil of Olay here! *"Sarah, you are just too beautiful"*, he tells her. *"Your beauty will be the death of me!"* Abraham would have made a great politician!

Therefore, he comes up with a story for Pharaoh that poses Sarah as his sister. (Every wife loves to be introduced as her husband's sister!) It wasn't totally untrue, of course. Sarah was actually his half-sister. But Abraham meant to scheme his way out of danger, and his lie worked. Not only did it work—it also seemed to pay off handsomely in terms of prosperity. The Egyptians accepted him and gave him livestock and servants (12:16). Materially, he was better off now than he was before. Sure, he had stretched the truth a bit; sure, he had put his family at risk. But wasn't it worth it in the end?

Just because things seem successful on the surface doesn't mean that God is pleased. I see heads of households making the same delusional mistakes today. They are driven to gain prosperity and climb the ladder of success—and they may even compromise their values on occasion, all in the name of being a good provider. Like Abraham, they have discovered that the world rewards handsomely for our service. But that prosperity comes at great price.

I can't imagine how difficult it must have been for Abraham to look again into Sarah's eyes. I can't imagine how challenging it must have been for Sarah to ever again hold him in as high respect as before. Forgiveness can come in any marred relationship. But trust is extremely difficult to rebuild.

As a consequence of Abraham's sin, the Lord punished the household of Pharaoh with diseases (12:17). We don't know how Pharaoh connected the plagues with his recent transaction with Abraham. Maybe Sarah told him. Regardless, Pharaoh immediately summoned Abraham and demanded an explanation (vv.18-19). You can hear the disgust in Pharaoh's words: "*If that's what it means to follow your God, I don't need it.*" Abraham's deceitful action has now been brought to light and his witness discredited. Abraham was embarrassed and also brought embarrassment upon the name of his God. He was called to be a blessing to all the peoples of the world. Sadly, he had instead brought a curse.

The Return Flight Back to Communion

I've been on some turbulent flights before, but none as bumpy as the one Abraham endured back to Canaan from Egypt. He had to retrace his steps back to Bethel (13:3). It was his last place of worship and it was beckoning his return. Abraham is spiritually bruised now, but the lessons that accompany those wounds will prove to be helpful later. At this point in time, he could not trust God to provide food in a famine. Yet Abraham will one day express to his soon-to-be sacrificed son "*the Lord will provide.*" Maybe the trip to Egypt had not been a total disaster after all.

By journeying back to Bethel, Abraham did what each of us must do in similar times of failure and doubt. We must retrace our steps back to where we last worshipped God. As the prophet Elisha asked the young man who had lost his borrowed ax head, "*Where did it fall?*" (2 Kings 6:1-7), so we must retrace our steps to the very place where last we lost communion with God.

Abraham acted out a requirement of spiritual communion: repentance. Repentance is a total change of direction. It's not continuing down the same wrong path hoping that it connects with the right road later. The wrong road taken in the midst of a bad decision never seems to turn into the right road. We must stop heading in the wrong direction and immediately retrace our steps back to the place where we made the fateful mistake. Retracing wrong steps is not easy. It requires a contrite spirit, a humble and submissive heart (Psalm 51:17). We must be willing to admit our stubborn failure and return once again to our Bethel. And because Abraham retraced his steps and went back, he found grace to start again and gain confidence in the God that he was only beginning to understand. One day, years later atop Mt. Moriah, he would know with complete confidence that God would always meet his needs—whether in a famine or on a mountaintop.

Is it possible that you have a bit of retracing to do? Maybe you've wandered from the time when you met with God on a regular basis and also trusted Him to meet your needs. It wasn't intentional, but you now realize that you're a long way from Bethel. Like Abraham, you've been living in a foreign culture that does not know God. Retrace your steps...God is waiting for your return. And like Abraham, returning to God doesn't mean the end of your troubles. We'll see in the next chapter that Abraham again faces another test—the test of security. Except this time, he is a bit wiser.

Trailnotes:

- Fear and faith are like the opposite ends of a seesaw; when one is up, the other is down.

- Our confidence in God is developed under stressful conditions. When was a time that adversity strengthened your faith?

- God builds our confidence in Him by first allowing us to lose confidence in ourselves.

- When we deliberately leave God's will, we assume the responsibility for our own outcome.

- Beware of making choices too quickly; it usually results in bad consequences.

CHAPTER 5
The Test of Security

"LOT LOOKED UP AND SAW THAT
THE WHOLE PLAIN OF THE JORDAN
WAS WELL WATERED, LIKE THE
GARDEN OF THE LORD...SO LOT
CHOSE FOR HIMSELF THE WHOLE
PLAIN OF THE JORDAN...THE TWO
MEN PARTED COMPANY."
(GENESIS 13:10-11)

Paul Harvey tells the story of a man named Henry who would often entertain guests in the evening. It was common to hear strange sounds at Henry's home—scratching sounds coming from beneath the floor. Everyone would usually pretend they didn't hear anything odd, even joking that he had ghosts when the sounds grew louder. But Henry knew the truth that lay just under his floor. After his guests would leave, Henry would take a lantern, open the trap door in his hall and descend the steps into the darkness of his cellar where his light would fall upon the face of a woman. The terrified woman, scared of the light, was chained to the wall. These were the days before mental institutions. People of this sort were cared for the best they could, though often locked in dark cellars. Night after night, Henry descended the steps to care for the woman in the cellar—his wife. In telling this story, Paul Harvey asked if Henry's situation could have prompted him before St. John's Church in 1775 to declare, "Is life so dear or peace so sweet as to be purchased at the price of chains? Forbid it, Almighty God!...I know not what course others may take, but as for me, give me liberty or give me death!" Henry was Patrick Henry. And as Harvey would so famously say, "Now you know the rest of the story!"[6]

So, what's in your cellar? What do you have hidden just under the surface of your life? Every so often, when no one else is around, you will visit it in that secret place that you hide so well. What is it that you are feeding with your time and attention? For Abraham, the source of his next downfall was his nephew, Lot.

As was true with Henry, whatever you have hidden in your cellar will often make enough noise to let you know that it's there. One day, you'll have to deal with

6   Paul Arandt, *Paul Harvey's the Rest of the Story*, Bantam Press, 1984.

it. It's like the carpet layer who was missing his cigarettes and happened to notice a lump in the carpet he had just laid down. Not wanting to go back and re-do his work just for a pack of cigarettes, he took a hammer and began to pound the lump until he had successfully smoothed it into submission. Later, he was a bit curious when he found his cigarettes under some extra carpet. About that time, a little boy came in with a rather worrisome look and said, "I can't seem to find my hamster, Mister. I left his cage door open and he's not there now. You haven't seen him, have you?"

In Genesis 13, the time has come when Abraham must deal with "his problem." Lot would force Abraham to make some difficult, life-altering decisions. But more importantly, God would use Lot to test Abraham's sense of security. Lot would press his uncle into deciding in whom or in what he would ultimately trust. The two men faced a crossroads because their herdsmen were quarreling with each other about whose land belonged to which master. The time had come when they must divide the land in this beautiful, new territory.

As he faces yet another test along the trail of transforming faith, we again have the advantage of knowing where this trail will lead him. Eventually he will stand on Mt. Moriah—secure in the confidence of God's provisions. However, there is an obstacle that lies in Abraham's transforming trail. It's called "security."

A Crisis Must be Faced Squarely

Our friend Abraham is no stranger to crisis. He faces yet another challenge, but there's a difference here. In the previous chapter, we see him dealing with the crisis of famine—a crisis that he didn't create. He had nothing to do with climate changes or high-pressure systems that prevent rain and cause drought. There are some crises that come from no fault of our own, but we must deal with them nonetheless. This new crisis is not something that has overtaken him as an innocent pawn in a cruel world. Like the lies he told in Egypt, this is a crisis of his own making. Let's break it down and examine the three sources of this crisis.

Crisis of Failure
So Abram went up from Egypt...and Lot went with him. (Genesis 13:1)

Abraham now enters this next test having returned from a sad chapter in his story of faith. We've all had similar chapters that we wish had never been written—chapters that came from a lack of confidence in God, prompted by impatience. Let's face it—we're not patient people either. We tend to be in a horn-honking, microwaving, Fed-Exing, emailing, fast food eating, express lane shopping hurry. We don't like waiting in traffic, on the phone, at the DMV or on our computer. Robert Levine, author of *A Geography of Time*[7], suggests the creation of a new unit of time—the smallest measure of time known to science—called a "Honko-Second." The "Honko-Second," he describes, is "the time between when the light changes and the person behind you honks his horn." Abraham faced a famine and then one "Honko-second" later, he was off to Egypt. Now licking his wounds, Abraham is a little older and a whole lot wiser. Thank God for the trip out of Egypt; thank God for the second chance!

---

7   Robert V. Levine, *A Geography Of Time: The Temporal Misadventures of a Social Psychologist,* Basic Books, 1998.

Crisis of Finance
Abram had become very wealthy... (Genesis 13:2)

You can't go to Egypt without bringing back some of Egypt with you. You can't leave God and enter into a land of faithlessness without bringing back a trunk load of souvenirs. As we've already seen, sometimes the world will reward us handsomely for our service. Abandoning your faith and going into a land of "sight," you always bring back some souvenirs—among them are sour attitudes, bad habits, a ruined witness and depressing guilt.

In Genesis 13, we find the first mention of personal wealth in the Bible. Wealth was one of the souvenirs Abraham brought back from Egypt. Wealth is not a sin, of course. But wealth does pose challenges that, if not handled correctly, can—and will—ruin us. Wealth gives us power, and the abuse of power can lead to ruin. Abraham's wealth would pose a test—a test of whether he would use his wealth and newfound power to get his own way or surrender his position for the benefit of another and trust his security with God.

Crisis of Friction
And quarreling arose between Abram's herdsmen and the herdsmen of Lot. (Genesis 13:7)

Riches can also lead to another crisis—friction between friends and family. Friction can sometimes be the result of disobedience. Remember, Abraham did not obey God's Word completely. As we've seen earlier, in his initial call to Abraham, God told him not to bring his family (Genesis 12:1). Lot was a family member that Abraham should have left behind. Partial obedience is total disobedience. By bringing him along, Abraham would pay the consequences.

I've watched in sad bewilderment how families get into a conflict after a funeral over the distribution of material possessions. Combine riches with character flaws, as in the case of Lot, and things get interesting! Abraham had carried Lot from Ur to Canaan in more than one way on this journey. Lot had benefitted greatly from Uncle Abe's prosperity—in fact, a lot of Lot's lot increased a whole lot! Now his flocks, livestock and herds began to compete with Abraham's for the same pastures and watering holes. Quarreling broke out between their herdsmen. For sure, it was a crisis of Abraham's making, but to his credit, he was willing to face the situation squarely and deal with this crisis head on.

Spiritual Choices Must Be Made

The situation between Abraham and Lot had reached a boiling point. Something had to be done. *"So Abram said to Lot, 'Let's not have any quarreling between you and me, or between your herdsmen and mine, for we are brothers. Is not the whole land before you? Let's part company. If you go to the left, I'll go to the right; if you go to the right, I'll go to the left'"*(Genesis 13:8-9).

This is a story about two men and two choices made according to two worldviews, with two completely different outcomes. Let's consider Lot for a moment and try to understand what was behind his choices because they reveal so much about his character.

Belief or Unbelief

Lot looked up and saw... (Genesis 13:10)

Abraham was obviously the elder, but he gave Lot

first choice. Much could be gathered from this simple gesture. For example, Abraham was developing his trust in God. By this time, he felt confident enough in God's provision that he didn't have to look after himself. He was in God's hands, and his offer to let Lot choose first was evidence of his growing faith.

On the other hand, we are told that Lot "*looked up and saw...*" (v.10). How much pain and anguish could Lot have spared for himself and others had he instead lifted his voice in prayer? But he lifted his eyes and saw "*the whole plain of the Jordan was well watered like the garden of the Lord.*" There is no indication that Lot's decision was based on anything resembling a relationship with God. It has often been said that the eyes are the window of the soul. Lot's eyes reveal a spiritual emptiness driven by a desire to fill the void of his life with things. A secular perspective, devoid of God, was all that motivated Lot.

However, before we judge him too harshly, we must admit that Lot probably decided as most of us make our decisions. We draw two columns on a sheet of paper and list the positives and the negatives regarding our options. Then we decide based on what column is the longest (funny how the "lust" list is always the longest!). Then after we decide, we pray and ask God to bless our decision. But such decisions are born out of unbelief.

Godliness or Worldliness
...like the land of Egypt... (Genesis 13:10)

Lot was also influenced by a worldly lust. Lot looked out over the attractive land option and saw, not just with his eyes, but also with his heart. The wording here reflects a longing of his heart. He was pursing an option that was attractive to his senses. Simply put, Lot was driven by lust. You could take Lot out of Egypt, but you couldn't take the Egypt out of Lot. Having tasted the fruits of Egypt when he was carried there by Uncle Abe, he well remembers the allure of the land and is drawn to return to something like it.

Many people, like Lot, have tasted Egypt and they struggle with a craving to return. Some struggle with the lingering effects of sin committed years ago, but it's hard to break loose from these sins. Although we can be forgiven of our past, the stain from the consequences of sin can stay with us all of our lives. These stains became embedded in our bodies and surface through addictions or obsessions. (This is part of the reason why even Christians can still struggle with various addictions.) We battle the patterns and habits that are embedded into the fabric of our bodies. That's why an alcoholic can be a Christian, but his body still craves another drink. That's why a drug addict can be a Christian, but her body still craves another fix. That's why a pornographer might be a Christian, but his mind still craves lust.

Add Satan into that mix and it results in a volatile situation. Satan knows what is embedded into the fabric of our bodies. He knows our trigger points. He knows what sets us off. He knows our weaknesses and our tendencies. He knows the taste we can develop for Egypt. That's why it's important to reach children early in life for Christ, before they travel too long in Egypt. For the longer one travels in Egypt, the deeper the stain left behind and the stronger the pull to replicate its pleasures.

Genesis 13:12 tells us that Lot settled near Sodom, one of the most wicked cities in the area. The places that offer us the best professional advantage are not always the best places to live. There are many times when we must work in secular environments that do not hold to our moral, social or spiritual values. Few of us have the luxury of working in a Christian environment. But that doesn't mean that we have to "live" among them. Lot knew the dangers of Sodom; he knew its reputation as a place of great wickedness. Yet Lot threw caution to the wind and moved there anyway. Lot reflects the approach of so many today. A secular, rather than a spiritual life perspective, fueled by lust, governed him. He made his choices primarily on the basis of professional advancement and social advantage. In doing so, he placed his family and his relationship with God in great jeopardy.

Selflessness or Selfishness
So Lot chose for himself... (Genesis 13:11)

Lot made decisions that put him in the best possible light. His choices were self-centered. However, we cannot place all the blame on Lot. After all, Lot learned from Uncle Abe how to make bad decisions. Didn't Abraham do exactly the same thing that Lot was now doing? When Abraham went to Egypt, wasn't it based on unbelief and worldly attraction? And once there, wasn't it pure selfishness that put Sarah in peril just to save his own neck? Abraham had gone through the exact same process of decision-making earlier. Now he must live with the sad consequences of seeing his bad example replicated in a family member. Lot had learned from his elder very well.

As a pastor for many years, I've seen this same sad scenario played out in many young people's lives. Parents have sat in my office, upset and hurt over a child's misbehavior. However, unfortunately, in many cases, these young people were merely mirroring the models they had observed for years.

Decision Making 101

What was Abraham's response to Lot's decisions? Now we begin to see some positive effects of Abraham's walk with God beginning to surface. Abraham's choices began reflecting his developing faith. We see his improved decision-making skills in at least two ways:

1) Abraham was concerned for his witness of God.

So Abram said to Lot, "Let's not have any quarreling between you and me, or between your herdsmen and mine, for we are brothers. Is not the whole land before you? Let's part company. If you go to the left, I'll go to the right; if you go to the right, I'll go to the left." (vv.8-9)

Abraham seemed to be more conscious now of the witness that he was giving to the world and how that witness might reflect upon God. He was not willing to create a scene that would reflect poorly on his God. This is a long way from where he once stood before the scolding voice of Pharaoh. Abraham didn't want to repeat that mistake. Fresh off ruining his testimony in Egypt, he took steps to preserve it here. He chose to preserve unity and peace in front of a watching community of his extended family and employees. Sadly, so much publicity has been focused on the mistakes highly placed Christian leaders have made that ruin their witness and soil God's name through their disunity and moral failure.

The world continues to watch with curious interest how God's people, called by His name, will live out that relationship in the context of their daily lives. That's why Paul says, *"Do everything without complaining or arguing, so that you may become blameless and pure, children of God without fault in a crooked and depraved generation, in which you shine like stars in the universe"* (Philippians 2:14-15).

2) Abraham was changed by the worship of God

From the Negev he went from place to place until he came to Bethel... and where he had first built an altar. There Abram called on the name of the Lord. (vv.3-4)

There are times when we simply go through the motions of worship. Our minds drift to places beyond... way beyond. As one who stands every week before a congregation, I know full well how this happens. I remember once while I was preaching seeing a fellow sitting near the front who was having a torturous time trying to stay awake. I noticed his head nodding forward. Then he would quickly arouse from slumber, lift his head and look around to see if anyone had noticed. He continued to fight the inevitable return of the dreaded sleeping nods when I noticed this time his head began to bob in a backward direction. Suddenly, he snapped his head forward with one quick jerk and his top dentures popped out. Like a snapping turtle, he quickly caught these misdirected dentures in midflight with his mouth! There he sat half-dazed, with his top dentures halfway sticking out of his mouth looking around to see if anyone saw this bit of dental gymnastics. I totally lost my train of thought and had to spend more than one uncomfortable moment finding my place in my notes so I could continue to preach. Needless to say, that was an unforgettable worship experience for me!

But Abraham's worship was unforgettable for another, more serious reason. When Abraham returned to Bethel, he "*called on the name of the Lord*" once more (13:4). Meeting God in such a dynamic moment before he faced Lot, Abraham began to reflect the character qualities that revealed why God wanted to use him in the first place. In the same manner, it is only in those moments of worship that we glimpse our full potential. Qualities like generosity, unselfishness, submission and patience were now evident in a man who so recently had failed so miserably. Having been previously burned by ill-advised impatience, Abraham is much slower now to respond. And when he does respond to Lot, his actions reflect the fact that Abraham had been with God.

Abraham's worship has now re-ordered his priorities. While it could be argued that wealth and even self-preservation had been his motivating influences before, he now sees life through a different lens. The things that once held sway over him don't seem to have the same influence because Abraham himself is not the same man.

Consequences Will Come Surely

Write this down (I'm serious! Go ahead, because it is a truth that you will see played out over and over in life): *"The choices we make will eventually make us."*

Every decision we make will return to us in the form of a consequence. You don't like your life? Don't like where you are at this point in your career? Don't like the person you married? Well, guess whose fault this is?

When we follow Lot's path, we see the sad digression of one becoming more and more acclimated to a wicked culture. In a pattern that is eerily reminiscent of the Garden of Eden, it started with an innocent, yet life-changing, look: *"Lot looked up and saw"* (v.10). But "looks" can be deceiving, especially when we are the ones doing the looking!

Next, we notice a further step in his digression: Lot pitched his tent *near* Sodom (v.12). Furthermore, we next find that his address has changed to a new home inside Sodom city limits (14:12). Lot now has a Sodom post office box. His "look" was settling into a steady gaze that slowly drew him deeper into Sodom's culture. Finally, we find him sitting at the gate of Sodom (19:1). This isn't a casual detail that describes him resting his feet. The city gate was the place where community leaders sat to transact city business during the day. This was where the city council met to conduct their meetings. Lot was more than a resident in this wicked environment; he was now a policy maker. Lot had become a leader. What started with a look is now a life.

A Life God Rewards

In contrast, if we follow Abraham's path, we see a much simpler story. He did not go the way of Lot. In fact, he picked up his tent and moved in a different direction near the "great trees of Mamre" (v.18). Encouraged, thankful and stronger, Abraham builds an altar and worships God once again. The prophet Isaiah would one day promise: "...*those who hope in the Lord will renew their strength. They will soar on wings like eagles; they will run and not grow weary, they will walk and not be faint*" (Isaiah 40:31).

Likewise, God is calling you into relationship with Him and to follow His call upon your life. He desires to use you and me for His grand purpose. But in order to be useful, you must have confidence in His provisions. You, too, must face the test of security.

At the conclusion of this story, Abraham's hope in the Lord is strengthened yet again—which is a good thing because he is going to need all the strength he can muster in the next chapter when he will endure a daring, life or death rescue of family members who find themselves embroiled in a heated conflict.

Trailnotes

- What you have hidden in your life will usually be exposed during crisis.

- Crises will come to each of us. Such times must be faced head on. How can you make sure that the choices you make during a crisis are aligned with your spiritual values?

- The choices we make reflect our character, and they have consequences!

- The choices we make will eventually make us.

CHAPTER 6

The Test of Success

¹² They also carried off Abram's nephew Lot and his possessions, since he was living in Sodom.

¹³ One who had escaped came and reported this to Abram the Hebrew. Now Abram was living near the great trees of Mamre the Amorite, a brother of Eshcol and Aner, all of whom were allied with Abram. ¹⁴ When Abram heard that his relative had been taken captive, he called out the 318 trained men born in his household and went in pursuit as far as Dan. ¹⁵ During the night Abram divided his men to attack

*them and he routed them, pursuing them as far as Hobah,
north of Damascus. ¹⁶ He recovered all the goods and brought
back his relative Lot and his possessions, together with the
women and the other people.*

*¹⁷ After Abram returned from defeating Kedorlaomer
and the kings allied with him, the king of Sodom came out to
meet him in the Valley of Shaveh (that is, the King's Valley).*

*¹⁸ Then Melchizedek king of Salem brought out bread
and wine. He was priest of God Most High, ¹⁹ and he blessed
Abram, saying,*

    "Blessed be Abram by God Most High,
    Creator of heaven and earth.
    ²⁰And blessed be God Most High,
    who delivered your enemies into your hand."
    (Genesis 14:12-20)

On June 27, 1976, members of the Palestine
Liberation Organization (PLO) and German
Revolutionary Cells hijacked an Air France plane
carrying 248 passengers. The terrorists forced the
plane to land in Entebbe, Uganda. Over the next
few suspenseful days, the hijackers would separate
the passengers into Israeli and non-Israeli hostages,
eventually releasing the 148 non-Israeli hostages. For a
week, the plane sat motionless with terrorists and 100
Israeli and Jewish passengers and the plane's pilot. Unless
their demands were met, all the remaining passengers
and pilot would be killed. The world waited nervously
for their next move.

Meanwhile, commandos of the Israel Defense
Forces (IDF) were preparing to make a daring attempt
at rescue. The IDF would not only prepare for a fight
with the terrorists but also anticipate resistance from
Uganda military forces. On July 4, Israeli transport

planes carrying 100 commandos over 2500 miles arrived in Entebbe under the cover of darkness. Operation Thunderbolt lasted 90 minutes and resulted in the successful rescue of all but three hostages. One Israeli commander was killed in the raid. All the hijackers and 45 Ugandan soldiers were killed also, and much of the Ugandan air force was destroyed.

Our next stop along Abraham's trail of transforming faith is a similar tale of war, heroism and rescue. Set against the backdrop of war, he will make a daring attempt to rescue a family member caught up in a regional conflict. The setting is modern day Iraq—where war continues to rage today. Armed conflict and war have dominated human history. The earliest of human records show soldiers with shields and helmets fighting in battle. Sadly, thousands of years have brought little change to our world.

Seeds of Conflict

In order to understand what led to Lot's demise, I need to share a little bit of backstory. Sodom, where Lot lived, was among the cities/states that paid tribute to the powerful King Kedorlaomer (let's call him "King K" for short) and his allies. For 13 years, these "Plain States" had paid taxes to the stronger "Kings of the East." This is the first mention of taxes given in the Bible. Additionally, this chapter is also unique in that it is also the first mention of the words: "war," "priest," "tithing," "bread" and "wine."

After 13 years of tax-burdens, they decided to lower taxes (their own!). They told King K about their new tax-reduction plan, and he responded as any good politician would respond to a tax-reduction plan—he didn't like it! King K called three other neighboring Kings of the East to ally with him and fight these Republicans—I mean "Plain States"—and muscle them back into submission.

The five tax-paying "Plain" Kings decided they would not be bullied. They realized the time had come to fight for what they believed. They were about to demonstrate a great principle of life: If you resist a bully, you better have the goods to back it up! They didn't. The "Kings of the Plains" were no match for these powerfully aligned, tax-hungry Kings of the East. King K and his forces easily annihilated the 5 Kings of the Plains. A leading Palestinian archeologist wrote of the devastation, "I found that every village in their path had been plundered and left in ruins, and the countryside left waste. The population had been wiped out or led away into captivity for hundreds of years thereafter, the entire area was like an abandoned cemetery hideously unkempt with all its monuments shattered and strewn in pieces on the ground."[8]

Guess who was in for a big tax hike? Lot was part of this collateral damage. The band of invading allies carted him off, along with all his possessions. There are those who might feel that Lot got what he deserved. Once again, we see that consequences have a way of showing up at the most inopportune moments. Lot's experience reminds us of how wonderful the grace of God is. Whether he realized it or not, Lot received another opportunity from God through this tragedy. He would be given another chance to get it right. Sadly, even this second chance would not result in a different outcome. Some people just will not learn.

8 Nelson Glueck, *Rivers in the Desert*, Farrar, Strauss and Cudahy, 1959, pp.72-73.

Calm is Often Interrupted by Disruptions that Force our Response (vv.13-16)

Abraham's life at this point is perfectly described by what Gordon MacDonald refers to as life's "disruptive moments." He settled in Canaan after the men chose their respective territories. Life was good...the rivalries that once divided his and Lot's clansmen were now quiet. It is usually in such unsuspecting and quiet moments that a crisis will crash in and disrupt our calm. Abraham was about to have a "disruptive moment" when a survivor of the devastating invasion by these Kings of the East made his way back to Abraham. Armed conflict had come to the area and Abraham's nephew and clansmen had become collateral causalities. Abraham was not looking for a fight...the fight had come to him.

There are some things worth fighting for. The life of righteous faith does not mean that we live a life of ease and passivity. As a matter of fact, the life of righteous faith may mean exactly the opposite! Abraham's bond to Lot was certainly born out of a blood relationship. I'm sure that Abraham felt responsible for the care of his brother's son. But Abraham's entry into battle is more than retaliation and rescue. Abraham lived in a state of readiness for battle. According to Scripture, there were 318 men "trained"—a clear indication of Abraham's readiness. Abraham reminds us by example what the Apostle Peter wrote, "*Be self-controlled and alert. Your enemy the devil prowls around like a roaring lion looking for someone to devour. Resist him, standing firm in the faith...*" (1 Peter 5:8-9).

I am greatly indebted, as are all Americans, to the U.S. military for their bravery and sacrifice. But whether physical, moral or spiritual, there are battles we must be willing to take up because it is the right thing to do. And once engaged, we must be prepared to win. When presented with a cause of right, Abraham did not hesitate to enter the battle. And being fully prepared and alert, he gains a great victory. Scripture says that he engaged the enemy, routed them all the way back north of Damascus and recovered all of Lot's stolen goods (Genesis 14:13-16).

Success Often Poses the Greatest Temptation (vv. 17, 21-24)

The greatest challenges to our faith will usually come not from vicious attacks, but victories; not from pain, but from popularity. If you had to choose, which would you rather experience—victory or defeat? Who wouldn't want to win? When have you ever heard an aspiring teen say, "One day I want be bankrupt and get fired from every job that I'm forced to work!"? Or, "I want to be homeless"?

While we know that bad things do happen to good people, and that failure sometimes comes to the most dedicated and sincere among us, the truth is that no one aspires to fail. In fact, our world is built around winning and those who win championships and gold medals. Quick! Who was the losing team in the last World Series? Actually, I'm not even sure who won it, but that's beside the point! Everybody wants to wear the team colors of a winner. Nobody wants to admit they pull for a loser. (That's why Duke fans only come out of hiding once a year!)

On the surface, a huge victory would appear to be a relatively secure place to be...safer than suffering and more pleasant than painful. But success is more complicated than it appears. Success often poses the greater risk. After his victory over Lot's enemies, Bera the king of Sodom approaches Abraham with a seemingly "unbeatable deal." With thanks for his daring rescue, Bera offers Abraham all the property he recovered from the four Kings of the East. *"Give me the people and keep the goods for yourself,"* he said (v.21). This was a tempting offer; after all, Abraham had risked his life—such a reward made sense. Abraham now faces the test of success square on—his character now weighs in the balance.

There are nuggets of sense and plausible reasoning that come with every temptation. It wouldn't be a temptation otherwise. There is no such thing as a temptation that doesn't sound reasonable. It is this pursuit of "reason"—this walk by sight—that is so contrary to faith. But fortunately for Abraham, he saw it for what it was: a temptation. He refuses the king's offer.

How to Escape from Temptation

How was Abraham able to defeat this temptation? Let me suggest three life lessons from this story.

First, Abraham had convictions *before* the encounter. *"But Abram said to the king of Sodom, 'I have raised my hand to the LORD, God Most High, Creator of heaven and earth, and have taken an oath'"* (Genesis 14:22). Notice Abraham speaks in past tense. Abraham had made an oath of faithfulness to God *in the past*, which allowed him to stand firm *in the present*. The moment of temptation is not the time to be developing convictions. If you don't have the right convictions before entering the "valley of temptation," you will likely not come out victorious. For young people on a date, the backseat of an automobile is no place to decide what you believe about morality and purity. Paul exhorts us, "...*offer yourselves to God, as those who have been brought from death to life; and offer the parts of your body to him as instruments of righteousness*" (Romans 6:13). The word "offer" here refers to a "once for all presentation." Having used the same word earlier in this same verse as a "continual action," Paul says, "*Stop continually offering the parts of your body as instruments of sin. Rather, make a once-and-for-all commitment that you will not now—or ever—offer another part of your body to sin*" (The Blanton translation). We should set firmly our escape route today, so we will be able to escape tomorrow when the pressure of temptation comes.

Second, Abraham had an understanding of the attachments that might come with the king's offer. Abraham refuses the king "*...so that you will never be able to say, 'I made Abram rich'*" (v. 23). For all his recent mistakes, let's at least give Abraham some credit here. At least he was wise enough to know things are usually more complicated than they first appear. Had he accepted this deal, he would have diluted the strength of his witness among his neighbors for future generations.

This was an offer from a king who ruled over a wicked and immoral city. There is every indication that he was no different in character than the people he ruled. Had his offer been accepted, Bera could have claimed that he helped "make Abraham." Such favors would create obligations to be cashed in later. Whenever his neighbors saw the future blessings of God on Abraham's life, they would have assumed that he got his start from the hand of a wicked king. Any potential blessings that might come to him would have been credited to Bera. God would have been robbed of glory.

Beware of the fine print that comes with each "reasonable" offer. The New Testament writer James says in James 1:14-15 that temptation can be compared to a fish swallowing a baited hook. What looks attractive at the moment can sometimes be spiritually fatal. At an earlier time, Abraham might have fallen for this ruse, but now he was learning to walk by faith, not sight. Walking by sight would have meant taking the money. But Abraham stood firm. He refused to be bought.

Third, Abraham made a firm response to the forbidden. He added to the king, "...*I will accept nothing belonging to you, not even a thread or the thong of a sandal...*"(v.23). He left no doubt where he stood. His response to Bera removed even the slightest hint of accepting this offer. Abraham was jumping from this cargo plane with no parachute. Sometimes we say "no," but we leave others in doubt as to what we really mean. Imagine Abraham saying, "*Oh, that's all right. That wouldn't be fair to you. I don't want to leave you empty-handed. You go ahead and keep it. If I ever get into a situation where I need anything, I'll call you.*" Such a response would have reflected a lack of faith in God's provisions.

Instead, Abraham removed any possibility that this man's wealth would be a viable option for him now, or for the future. He left no doubt. It takes courage to speak with such clarity and conviction. This kind of response can't come packaged in hesitancy or reluctance to hurt someone's feelings. The message must be clear: "*This is something I simply cannot do!*"

God Prepares and Strengthens Us for Temptation (vv.18-20)

Abraham seemed unusually clear and forceful in his response to Bera's offer, don't you think? Where did he find that inner guiding compass? Let's go back in the story to see. Shortly before his seductive offer from Bera, Abraham made acquaintance with another king (Genesis 14:18-20). This king, Melchizedek his name, is one of the most mysterious figures in the entire Bible. He seems to appear out of nowhere, and just as mysteriously, he disappears. He blessed Abraham and Abraham responded by giving him a tenth of all his possessions.

Melchizedek is only mentioned here and in two other places in Scripture. One thousand years after this occasion, the psalmist would refer to him in Psalms 110:4 as a type of priest to be fulfilled by the Lord's anointed One. But it would be the writer of Hebrews, another thousand years beyond that, who would more fully develop the symbolic role of this mysterious one.

Many commentators are divided over the identity of Melchizedek. There are those who believe that he was the pre-incarnate Christ. There are at least three reasons for this conclusion:

- The name "Melchizedek" actually means "righteousness of God."
- He was identified in title as "King of Salem" (Salem means "city of peace.") You may recognize "Salem" as being the place that will one day be known as "Jerusalem."
- His role was that of priest—mediator with God.

The combination of his royal position (king) and his priestly position makes Melchizedek an attractive representation of our Lord Jesus Christ. As priest, Christ brought atonement with God by offering His own body as our sin sacrifice. In so doing, Christ is our perfect mediator (1 Timothy 2:5). And as our resurrected Lord, He will one day return as the King of Kings (Revelation 19:16). Whether Melchizedek was actually a pre-incarnate visitation of Christ or not, I don't know. As easy as it would be to assume that this was Christ, maybe the actual truth is that he was a priestly king who would serve as a prototype of the role that Christ would one day come to fulfill. Regardless of his exact identity, the greater fact here is that Abraham was encouraged by his ministry.

In the Gospel of John, Jesus makes an interesting statement regarding Abraham. He says, "*Your father Abraham rejoiced at the thought of seeing my day; he saw it and was glad*" (John 8:56). Have you ever wondered *when* Abraham saw such a day? It's entirely possible that this scene in Genesis was *when* Abraham saw Christ and the ministry that He would one day bring to the world. We are told that Melchizedek brought out bread and wine. There in King's Valley 2000 years before the Upper Room Service, Abraham was "seeing the day" of Christ. The same elements Jesus would one day share with His disciples and say, "*This is my body which is broken for you…This is my blood which is shed for you*" are the same elements shared between Abraham and this "priest of God Most High."

We cannot know the full impact and sacredness of this moment for Abraham. But we can see the results in his upcoming encounter with Bera. More and more, we glimpse the formation of a faith that will one day be clearly demonstrated on Mt. Moriah. Yet, we get ahead of ourselves. There is still much refining and growth that must take place before we get to that sacred place.

The lessons learned in this valley called Shaveh will serve Abraham well on that sacred mountain.

Christ's Ministry to Us

Just as Abraham received prior strength for his encounter with Bera by the sacred communion that took place with Melchizedek, so Christ wants to draw near to strengthen us in our time of temptation. The sacrifice of Christ, symbolized by the bread and wine in this story, is our encouragement for strength as well. His death on the cross was my sacrifice of past sin, and His resurrection is my strength over present sin. Genuine worship that reflects on this wonderful reality is my key to success over any temptation that follows. Don't neglect those moments with God. He has provided a way for our victory and it is through Christ.

The lure of seductive offers would not sway Abraham to relinquish his trust in God. Holding God firmly by faith, he willingly released whatever else was in his hands. As evidence of this, we are told that Abraham gave Melchizedek "a tenth of everything" (v.20). Hundreds of years before tithing was written as a law, God wrote it on the heart of a grateful servant. When God dramatically grips the heart of a servant, whatever else was previously held dear is willingly and lovingly released. That's why tithing is not a material issue, but a spiritual one. A person who meets God in authentic worship will gladly give back a tithe of what God has allowed him or her to gain. Abraham's walk of faith is gaining momentum now. His pace is picking up. The greatest indicator of our spiritual reliance is how we manage our resources. Abraham's gift gave evidence of his walk with God—it always does.

Looking Ahead

At this point, Abraham had soundly passed the test of success. He rescued his nephew and defeated the forces that kidnapped him, while resisting the lure of a financially seductive offer. Finally, he then experienced the exhilaration of being personally encouraged by a renowned and highly regarded priest, Melchizedek. This chapter of his life had been quite eventful, and it would appear to us—successful. However, the next chapter in this story begins with the ominous words: *"But after this..."* (15:1). After all the victories, after the lights are all out and the parking lot is empty, Abraham was alone. It was in this moment of aloneness that he struggled with fear and self-doubt.

Trailnotes

- Life is often interrupted by "disruptive moments"—expect them!

- Our greatest challenges often come from our successes. When was a time this proved to be true in your life?

- Our response to temptations must be decisive and clear.

- Beware of the "fine print" that comes with attractive offers. It was through the strengthening ministry of a priestly-king that Abraham was able to resist an alluring offer. Remember, our strength comes from Christ, our Priest and King.

CHAPTER 7

The Test of Inner Struggle

¹After this, the word of the Lord came to Abram in a vision:

"Do not be afraid, Abram. I am your shield, your very great reward."

² But Abram said, "O Sovereign Lord, what can you give me since I remain childless and the one who will inherit my estate is Eliezer of Damascus?" ³ And Abram said, "You have given me no children; so a servant in my household will be my heir."

⁴ Then the word of the Lord came to him: "This man will not be your heir, but a son coming from your own body will be your heir." ⁵ He took him outside and said, "Look up at the heavens and count the stars—if indeed you can count them." Then he said to him, "So shall your offspring be." (Genesis 15:1-5)

I'll never forget watching "The Wizard of Oz" for the first time. My family and I had stayed home one Sunday night from church. As I recall, I watched most of that movie from behind my chair. I was gallantly hanging in there until those flying monkeys began to disassemble the Scarecrow. That's when I told my kids to turn it off because I couldn't take it anymore!

Our study of Abraham reminds me of a significant moment in that movie when Dorothy and her friends fearfully faced the awesome Wizard. Toto, unfazed by the reputation and the thundering presentation of the Wizard, pulls back the curtain and exposes the truth about the Wizard. He was totally human. The awe-inspiring respect given to the Wizard was based on embellished reputation. With the truth fully exposed, the Wizard seemed very vulnerable. In our story about Abraham, the curtain has likewise been pulled back, and now we get a glimpse of Abraham that we've not seen before.

I tread carefully here. I do not at all suggest that Abraham's reputation was "smoke and mirrors." Nor do I suggest that his sterling reputation was undeserved. Not for one moment. In fact, Abraham's faith was so significant that God would use that faith as the basis upon which all human faith would be measured. Abraham was deserving of his induction into the Faith Hall of Fame (Hebrews 11). But it should also be noted that Abraham was no Superman either. When the curtain is pulled back in the biblical story about him, we see him more completely as human and vulnerable. This shouldn't diminish our opinion of him, but rather it can heighten our admiration of him.

As Genesis 15 opens, we see God having to comfort Abraham and reassure him that He had no reason to be afraid. Although he had just experienced an enormous victory, he is struggling with such fear and self-doubt that God must calm his fears and remind him of His strength. Remember, Abraham still wasn't totally settled in his new land—and he didn't even have a son through whom God's blessing would come. What was next in God's plan for Abraham? Abraham didn't know.

God Knows Exactly How We Feel (Genesis 15:1a)

There are several lessons that we learn from Abraham in this humanizing moment of inner struggle—the first of which is that God understands our emotions. The phrase "After this..." opens Genesis 15 and it is a connecting phrase that ties together the exciting events of the previous chapter's battle with the conversation God and Abraham are now having.

After the elation of chapter 14 comes the depression in chapter 15. There is no mention that Abraham ever cried out to God, no record of him pouring out his depressed thoughts. The text simply says God showed up and knew exactly what he was going through without Abraham having to explain. Likewise, it is not unusual to find yourself struggling with thoughts of failure and inadequacy, especially in the aftermath of victory. Neither is it unusual to look for some flaw regarding our relationship with God. We wonder if we've failed Him or if He has forsaken us.

This scene reminds me of another of God's servants, Elijah. Having experienced the dramatic victory on Mt. Carmel against the prophets of Baal, he immediately lapsed into a depression so deep that he wanted God to kill him (1 Kings 19:4-14). Elijah's response has always been a curiosity to me. It's a good example of how distorted our mental reasoning can be during depression. If Elijah really *wanted* to die, why did he run from Jezebel? He could have just stayed on Mt. Carmel and Jezebel would have gladly done that for him! When one is physically and emotionally exhausted, irrational thoughts are common. It is natural for us to go through periods of emotional intensity and then suffer the draining results, both in terms of mental fatigue and physical exhaustion. Emotional highs are usually always followed by emotional lows. It is in such moments that we are the most vulnerable to failure.

I've gained a lot of encouragement from observing Abraham. When I see him struggle in the wake of victory, I see so much of myself. Hardly a week goes by that I don't wrestle with this monster. There are times when I think that I am winning the struggle, but then I'll face an unexpected setback. A sense of failure and worthlessness floods my mind, and I'm left with questions that God seems silent to answer.

Don't get me wrong. I count it a great privilege to serve in a church with a lot of exhilarating moments. For me, almost every Sunday is an adrenalin rush. The butterflies start on Saturday afternoon and slowly build until I stand up to preach. But there is another side of that reality for me. After the last service is over and the last hand is shaken, the parking lot is empty and the lights are out—that's when the real battle begins for me. I go home through a dark valley. I don't know where it comes from and I can't explain it, but I only know it hurts. I've been told that it was chemical in origin—my body trying to adjust back to "normal" (whatever that is!). But getting the exact diagnosis isn't the most important matter. Regardless of where it comes from, it still comes across as spiritual failure. Physical causes notwithstanding, Satan has tried to cash in on those moments to overshadow the blessings. It seems that the greater the victory on Sunday, the darker the Monday. I've jokingly said that I've written many resignation letters on Mondays, only to tear them up on Tuesdays. Still, in that jest there's a nugget of truth.

Pulling back the curtain to expose a vulnerable side of me is not something that I relish doing. However, I realize there are many others who relate to what I've described. You have your own dark struggles that you keep locked inside—too afraid or embarrassed to let anyone know. Like you, I search for answers in those dark moments. However, it is in those moments that I've come to better appreciate what Abraham found to be true: God knows exactly how we feel.

God is the Solution to What I Face (Genesis 15:1b)

At his most vulnerable point, Abraham heard God's clear assurance—*"Do not be afraid."* This is the first of many times that this phrase will echo across the pages of the Bible. Isaac, Joshua, Gideon, Daniel, Joseph and Mary, the shepherds in Bethlehem, the women at Jesus' empty tomb—all these received the same comforting assurance, *"Do not be afraid."* If you are in a fearful place in your life right now, consider your situation in light of these saints of God throughout history.

At this point along the trail of transformation, Abraham encountered a glimpse of God never before seen by anyone. He was meeting for the first time the great "I AM." Moses would later meet the great "I AM" in the Egyptian desert (Exodus 3). However, Abraham was the first to witness the disclosure of God's unique character upon humanity. The "I AM" would remove some of the mystery surrounding the God that called out to Abraham and beckoned his obedience. Here, God takes a grand giant step toward identifying Himself and says, "*I AM—your shield. I AM—your great reward.*"

The great unknowable and invisible God now reveals Himself in knowable and visible concepts that Abraham and others can understand. Of course, the "I AM" that is self-disclosed to Abraham, and later to Moses, would only be a preview of what was to come. The "I AM" would find its ultimate fulfillment in Christ Jesus as witnessed in the gospels.

"I am your shield"

A shield is a barrier of protection between you and whatever poses a threat to your wellbeing. When the blows come and the arrows fly, a good shield is strong enough to repel them. Abraham had just emerged from a battle against four powerfully allied kings—he knew well the importance of a shield. After the dust had settled and he reflected upon his immediate accomplishments, I wonder if Abraham thought to himself, "What was I thinking?" Sure Abraham won, but now he faces retaliation! Have you ever done something courageous and later reconsidered your sanity? Dangers now seen in the light of day sometimes make us realize in retrospect that our course of action probably wasn't the safest...or wisest...one.

As I said before, there are battles worth fighting. There are principles and people precious to us worth fighting for, but those victories often come with backlashes. The fear of reprisal can be crippling. Yet when we've fought the good fight—done the right thing— God positions Himself between us and any threat. He is our shield. God positioned Himself between Abraham and those who threatened him harm. Any king bent on retaliation would have to go through God to get to Abraham. What is it that poses threat or danger to you? Let the words of the psalmist be a confident and reassuring hope for you.

> *"My God is my rock, in whom I take refuge,*
> *my shield and the horn of my salvation.*
> *He is my stronghold, my refuge and my savior—*
> *from violent men you save me.*
> *I call to the LORD, who is worthy of praise,*
> *and I am saved from my enemies."* (2 Samuel 22:3-4)

"I am your very great reward"

The second way God describes Himself is Abraham's "very great reward." Just a short while ago, Abraham refused a reward for returning the plundered property taken by the Kings of the East. Again, we don't know the exact nature of Abraham's inner struggle, but perhaps he was having second thoughts about such actions. In hindsight, he might have wondered, "Maybe I shouldn't have been so quick to turn that down. I may really need that later."

In our own moments of doubt and uncertainty, God says, "*I AM…your very great reward.*" In other words, "Abraham, you've got Me. And when you have Me, you have your great reward." The most precious reward in life is not something we hold in our hands, but in our hearts. For faithful service, God will reward us with Himself and in greater proportions than the worldly rewards we may accumulate. And when we have the great "I AM," we have all that God is. Is God wise? We share that wisdom. Is God holy? We share in that holiness. Is God almighty? We share in that power.

God Challenges Me to Look Up (Genesis 15:5)

What was really weighing on Abraham the most was the fact that he still did not have a son. The fear of being childless was a weight that seemed too heavy to bear. The fear of leaving no descendants to carry on one's work and identity was a burden that may be hard to understand completely in our day.

However, for Abraham and others in the biblical record, it was powerful. Even though God had promised him a son, Abraham didn't yet have him. Other than God's promise, there was no further indication that he ever would have him. With each passing day, the fulfillment of that promise grew dimmer. Abraham needed a lift. And he got one. God told him to go out and lift up his eyes to the heavens. *"He took him outside and said, 'Look up at the heavens and count the stars—if indeed you can count them.' Then he said to him, 'So shall your offspring be'"* (Genesis 15:5).

Look away from the Source of Your Doubt

When Abraham looked down, what did he see? He saw an old man far beyond the age of reproduction. He saw a wife who had never borne children and now, at roughly age sixty-five, chances were not looking too good for that to ever change. As long as Abraham looked down, he was discouraged by what he saw. Looking down, he saw doubt. Looking down, he saw an impossible situation. Looking down, he didn't measure up—he wasn't good enough. We struggle with self-doubt and feelings of inferiority when we see our weaknesses and failures. We fixate on the limitation of others to make us happy and fulfilled. When we do these things, we are looking in the wrong direction! The first thing God did to address Abraham's doubt was to readjust his focus by telling him to *"look up"* and get his eyes off of his situation.

Stretch Your Mind to See the Greatness of God

God took him outside and gave him a different perspective—one much greater than he saw in his situation. As Abraham gazed toward the eastern sky, the stars were so clear that it seemed he could reach up and touch them. Then God told him to count them. Could you count the stars? Hardly. It was an impossible exercise. This exercise stretched Abraham's perspective of God and reminded him that he could not even count what God, in His awesome greatness, had already named (Job 38).

God was saying, "If I hung all those stars in an orderly course in the vast reaches of the heavens...if I have given them names...don't you think I'll be able to provide at least one heir for you?" I doubt if there was ever another night that Abraham did not look up at the heavens and remember God's promise. I think that was a life-changing moment for Abraham. The inner struggle of his soul had been quieted. What Abraham takes away from that eventful night will influence him forever. No doubt, it prepared him to face one of the toughest tests yet—the test of trust. In the next chapter, we'll see how a hopeless situation on the trail of transforming faith threatened to derail him. However, Abraham's unexpected show of great faith made all the difference.

Trailnotes

- God knows exactly how you feel.

- What is your greatest need right now? God meets that need by saying, "I AM."

- When you are doubtful and worried about your future, God says, "Look up!" Looking up, we look away from the source of our doubts and look upon the size of His greatness.

CHAPTER 8
The Test of Trust

"*Abram believed the Lord, and he credited it to him as righteousness.*"
(*Genesis 15:6*)

D r. J. Harold Smith is the voice of "The Radio Bible Hour," a program heard for over 75 years. Dr. Smith was from my hometown of Woodruff, South Carolina. He once returned to Woodruff when I was eight years old to preach a series of revival messages in my church, which changed the course of my life. After listening to his fiery messages all week, on Saturday night I could withstand the force that was pounding in my heart no longer. I don't remember the finer details of that night except that I could not hold back the flood of tears that seemed to pour forth when I stepped forward during the invitation.

I didn't understand much about God at that moment, but I felt in my heart His calling and knew that I could resist Him no longer. I'm reminded of a familiar verse in the hymn *Amazing Grace*: "How precious did that grace appear, the hour I first believed."

After God explained once more that Abraham would indeed become the father of many nations, the Bible simply says Abraham "believed" (15:6). In our New Testament vernacular, I believe this was the moment Abraham was saved. The moment he "believed," the result was righteous standing with God.

Right standing with God has always been granted on the same basis for all of humanity—by grace through faith (Ephesians 2:8, 9). The fact that God is the same yesterday, today and forever (Hebrews 13:8) makes this truth clear. Paul also emphasizes this principle in his letter to the Romans. The basis of salvation was set *before* the Law and the Jewish nation were ever born. Pointing back to the pre-Law time of Abraham, Paul reminds us that Abraham's fulfillment of God's promises came as a result of grace through faith (Romans 4:16).

The faith Abraham expressed in verse 6 marks a

dramatic turning point on the trail. We're not sure how much time elapses between God's reassuring promise of (v.5) and Abraham's step of faith (v.6). Maybe it was immediate. Perhaps some weeks went by and, like my story, he wrestled with the pounding within his own chest. But finally, "Abraham went forward during the invitation," placed his faith in God and was saved.

Abraham Believed God in the Absence of Proof

If faith is an indispensable element of being right with God, several features of Abraham's faith are worth noting. In the face of insurmountable evidence to the contrary, Genesis 15:6 says he "*believed.*" The word refers to being firmly, completely, 100% convinced that something is true, even though it is not yet true and there is no evidence that it ever will be true! It is similar in function to our idea of "Amen," which means, "so be it." (Where I grew up, it was "Aaaaamen!" It wasn't until seminary that I realized the word had only one "a" in it.) Abraham "Aaaaamened" what God said with his life. Paul would look upon Abraham's faith and comment: "*Against all hope, Abraham in hope believed.., Without weakening in his faith, he faced the fact that his body was as good as dead— since he was about a hundred years old—and that Sarah's womb was also dead*" (Romans 4:18-19).

What makes Abraham's statement of his faith so special was his limited understanding of God at that time. Think about it: his knowledge of God was still very minimal. He knew God had said He would give him Canaan as an inheritance for the offspring that would make him a father of a great nation. Yet, ten years have passed since God originally issued this promise (12:2-3) and still there was no evidence (none, nil, nada, zip, zero, zilch!) that what God had promised was ever going to come true. Abraham was still living in a tent, and he didn't own a single square foot of land. Regarding a son, he wasn't getting any younger and Sarah (bless her heart!) wasn't looking up to the task either! Hope was getting scarce.

Imagine if Abraham had gone before a judge and asked what the chances might be. The judge would want to examine the evidence. I imagine the interaction might go something like this:

"Well, Mr. Abraham, we've never seen God do anything like this before. There's no historical precedent."

"No, sir. You're right about that."

"Besides, you are obviously beyond child-bearing age! Abraham, how old are you?

"Eighty-five, sir."

"And your wife Sarah...isn't she seventy-five? I've made my point! Do you really think this is going to happen? And if for some miraculous reason that it did happen, do you want to become a freak of nature among your neighbors?"

"Well...."

"...Add to all this, even *if* your wife did conceive, she probably would die during childbirth. It seems more logical that God could accomplish all this in a much simpler way if that is what He really wanted to do!" The presiding judge would then likely throw out the case.

This becomes the critical point in Abraham's story, and for that matter the rest of the Bible. So what does Abraham do? *Abraham believed the Lord, and [God] credited it to him as righteousness.* Another 15 years would pass before the promise would finally be fulfilled. That would make Abraham 100 years old and Sarah 90, which would certainly make them the oldest couple in the

Lamaze class!

Are you willing to "amen" God's promises to you? Would you dare say to God, "The plans you have for me, as unbelievable as they may seem to others, 'let it be so' as you have said. I'm willing to trust you!"?

Abraham's Faith Was Made Strong Because He Believed in a Strong God

Romans 4:20-21 says, "*Yet he did not waver through unbelief regarding the promise of God, but was **strengthened** in his faith and gave glory to God, being fully persuaded that God had **power** to do what he had promised.*" The words "strengthen" and "power" come from the same root word meaning, "*a continuous source of power.*" In other words, Abraham's faith grew in strength because he was fully 100% convinced that God's power was continually at work to bring about what He had promised. Abraham's faith was empowered by focusing his attention on God's power. The more he thought about God, the more convinced ("*fully persuaded*") he was that God could do whatever He promised.

Herein lies the secret of faith: *The strength and worth of one's faith is determined by the strength and worth of the object of that faith.* Your faith is no stronger than *where* you place that faith. Much faith can't overcome a faulty object. The object must be reliable. "[Abraham]...*was strengthened in his faith and gave glory to **God**, being fully persuaded that **God** had power to do what he had promised*" (Romans 4:20-21). The object of Abraham's faith was in an all-powerful God who had hung the stars in the sky.

I hear often the remark, "You've just got to have faith!" Or, "I believe that it is going to happen. I just know that it will," as if the sheer magnitude and intensity of one's faith will bring it to pass. That's an example of having faith in faith. Faith is the object of that sort of faith and it is faulty. It's not much different than those who have strong faith in thin ice. (I'd love to ask them about this, but none of them are around!) Technically, they died in faith. And truth be told, they may have had a lot of it. Yet, their faith could not save them. Why? The object of their faith was weak; therefore, their faith brought weak results.

Your faith is only as good…only as strong…as the object in which it is placed. There is nothing in Abraham alone that gave him strong faith, but everything in God made his faith strong. When God saw that Abraham viewed Him as powerful and trustworthy and put his faith in His power to fulfill His promises, that's when God *"credited it to him as righteousness."*

Abraham's Faith is a Model for All Who Desire to be Right with God

By faith, Abraham said in effect: *"Lord, I believe You. I believe You are powerful enough to do all the things You've said. Though I am powerless, You are all powerful and I will rest in that. I will live not in the light that I see, but in light of what You have said."*

When God saw that faith, He responded in effect: *"Abraham, your faith has united us. You see things as I see them. I forgive all your sins and receive you into My presence. Your faith has become the standard by which I want all people to trust Me. Anyone who believes in Me as you have done will be righteous in My sight."* Abraham was still guilty of sin, as we all are. His statement of faith, as dramatic as it was, still did not remove the sin of his past. Like all of humanity, Abraham needed a Savior. Abraham would be "saved forward," made righteous by a sacrifice some 2000 years in the future; it is the same sin sacrifice upon which we look back 2000 years and are saved.

Abraham's faith is a model for us in that his faith grasped two key concepts about God. The Apostle Paul supplied the insight in Romans 4:17: "...*in whom [Abraham] believed—the God who gives life to the dead and calls things that are not as though they were.*" Two concepts that are vital in saving faith are mentioned here:

1. Abraham believed God "gives life to the dead."

This was remarkable, for there was no recorded resurrection at this point in history. No doctrine of resurrection revealed by God; no past precedent on which to base this hope. This was new ground. Abraham must have looked into the heavens and reasoned, "If God is powerful enough to create the stars and hang them in the sky and give them an orderly course, then surely He is powerful enough to raise the dead." This would ultimately be borne out on Mt. Moriah when he would put this trust into practical obedience by being willing to sacrifice Isaac, knowing that God could give him back by raising the dead if He so desired. It was an amazing step of faith.

2. Abraham saw God as One who "calls things that are not as though they were."

In other words, Abraham saw God as one who "*creates out of nothing.*" The opening verse of the Bible sets forth this truth ("*In the beginning God **created** the heavens and the earth*"). God started with nothing and created something from it. Only God can do that and Abraham believed this truth! For all practical purposes, giving Abraham and Sarah a son would be like creating something out of nothing. Abraham believed that God could take nothing (and let's be honest, that's all God had to work with here!) and make it into something. Both Abraham and Sarah could offer nothing. If God was ever going to fulfill His promise, Abraham knew that God was going to have to reach into the nothingness of his and Sarah's reproductive potential and create something from nothing. If God was going to do it, He would have to create a son for Abraham and Sarah the same way that He created the sun in the heavens ...out of nothing!

How to Have Transforming Faith

If you are ever to be in a right relationship with God, you must possess a faith that grasps the same following two elements represented in Abraham's faith:

First, you must believe that God can raise the dead. He did just that when He raised Jesus from the dead. Jesus *"was delivered over to death for our sins"* (yours, mine, Abraham's) *and was raised to life* (to verify that God accepted what Christ had offered) *for our justification"* (Romans 4:25, parentheses added). Every person must, as Romans 10:9 says, *"Confess with your mouth, 'Jesus is Lord,' and believe in your heart that God raised him from the dead"* in order to be saved.

Second, you must bring a humble spirit before God that admits your empty condition. We must bring to Him the empty attitude that says, "God, if You wish to do anything in my life, it will have to come from You because I have nothing to offer!" We must come just like the psalmist who pleaded, *"Create* (out of nothing!) *in me a clean heart, O God"* (Psalm 51:10, parentheses added). When our hearts are stained with sin, we have nothing to offer. Once we exercise our faith, the words of the classic hymn ring true for us:

Amazing grace! How sweet the sound,
that saved a wretch like me!
I once was lost, but now am found,
was blind but now I see.
'Twas grace that taught my heart to fear,
and grace my fears relieved;
How precious did that grace appear
the hour I first believed!

And now we are inching our way closer to the Mt. Moriah experience for which God had been preparing Abraham all along. However, before that moment, there is one more test. And this one seems very unexpected. Just when Abraham most needed to hear from God, all he heard was silence. In the next chapter, we'll see how devastating this experience of silence can be.

Trailnotes

- Faith is an indispensable element of being right with God. How do you demonstrate that you trust God?

- Abraham's faith grew in strength. How do you know if you have a growing faith?

- Your faith is only as strong as the object in which it is placed.

- Abraham was willing to "amen" God's promises with his life. How willing are you to do the same thing?

- Faith is the absence of evidence. Abraham believed God's promises even though there was no evidence to prove they would ever be fulfilled.

- Two pillars supported Abraham's faith: 1) Believing that God can raise the dead 2) Believing that God can create something out of nothing.

CHAPTER 9
The Test of Silence

"NOW SARAI, ABRAM'S WIFE, HAD
BORNE HIM NO CHILDREN..."
(GENESIS 16:1)

In the movie, *Shine*, a young man's life is crushed under the oppression and abuse of a highly possessive father. When his mind could no longer accept the strain, it unraveled and he was institutionalized for years. Later, at a better time in life, he looks back on all that has happened and reflects, "I guess I didn't grow up; I grew down."[9]

I can't count the number of times that I've come to the same conclusion about myself. As I read about the turn of events in Genesis 16, I can see that it was true of Abraham also. The story of Abraham is a story of growing up...and growing down. In fact, the reason Abraham is so dear to us is that he mirrors our own journey of faith. It's encouraging to see that even the Old Testament's greatest figure failed at times, just as we do. As we once again join Abraham in his transforming journey of faith, we find him facing yet another test—a test Abraham will fail. In failing the test, he will "grow down."

Sometimes God Is Silent

One of the toughest places we can ever be is in the midst of God's silence. These times of silence shouldn't surprise us, however, because the dynamics of faith require them. You can't have faith in the absence of silence. Job knew this place well; so did the psalmist. (As you read through the Psalms, notice how often the psalmist cries out for God to answer!) Most of the beloved characters in the Bible endured agonizing periods of God's silence. Even Jesus cried out from the cross for the Father to break His silence. Silence is an issue that all of God's servants wrestle with at times. So it was with Abraham. At this point in

---

9   Gordon MacDonald, *Mid-Course Correction*, Thomas Nelson Publishers, 2005, p.125

the story, it had been 10 years since Abraham heard the "Voice." Ten years without being reassured that he was doing the right thing. Ten years of silence.

Silence is one of the most challenging places servants of God find themselves because it tests the worth and confidence of the object in which we've placed our trust. Silence is an uncomfortable place to be. We're not geared for it. We want answers, we desire direction, we need help and we thirst for encouragement...but we only get *silence!* There is an episode in Abraham's faith transformation that helps bring this into focus for us when he and Sarah circumvent God's plan and have a baby with Hagar, their servant, so Abraham could have an heir. We are reminded not only of how vulnerable we all are to doing our own thing in times of silence but also of how harmful the results are when we fail to respond in faith.

In the Midst of Silence, Be Careful Whose Voice You Follow

The silence of God exposes vulnerability in a servant of God. We want to *do* something. We want to know that we are making progress and moving meaningfully down the road of accomplishment. The last thing Abraham heard from God 10 years earlier was that "*from your own body will be your heir*" (Genesis 15:4). Well, being approximately eighty-five years of age doesn't seem to hold the optimal advantage in seeing that promise fulfilled! Perhaps Abraham reasoned that God needed help.

It's interesting how much trouble we get into when we try to help God. Up until now, Abraham had been listening to "the Voice." However, Abraham's attention has now been directed toward another voice—

that of Sarah who suggests that he sleep with their servant (16:2).[10] When God is silent, we are tempted to go searching for other voices to fill the void. Beware of the voices to which you listen. Where do you get your counsel? What sources shape your values?

The most dangerous voices sometimes come from those who love us the most. To her credit, I believe Sarah loved Abraham. She cared deeply about his disappointments. While no one is totally removed from his or her own selfish motives, I believe she was motivated by love when she comes up with this idea. As such decisions usually go, however, it will turn out to be a painfully divisive plan.

Hagar was from Egypt, the place of Abraham's ill-advised detour years earlier (Genesis 12:10ff). Hagar was one of the "souvenirs" that Abraham brought back for Sarah when he went to Egypt. Some wives get t-shirts or salt and pepper shakers when their husbands return from a trip; Sarah got Hagar. Did you notice that the fruit of a bad decision keeps coming back? We've already seen what Egypt represents in the life of faith: abandoning God and doing our own thing—walking by sight rather than faith. Although now it is many years later, the time Abraham spends in Egypt comes back to haunt him yet again. Once more, we see that you can't go into Egypt without bringing some of Egypt back with you.

There is a hint of disappointment and resignation in Sarah's voice as she unfolds her offer. *"The Lord has kept me from having children. Go, sleep with my maidservant"* (16:2). Sarah reasons somehow that God is behind her barrenness. It is His fault! When we believe that God is behind our problems, we feel much more justified offering our own human solutions. In a conversation eerily similar

10   Ibid. p.85

118

to that between Adam and Eve in the Garden of Eden, Sarah presents a bitterly seductive fruit and Abraham willingly takes a bite. It would be a mistake the world would live to regret.

How could a man, noted in his past for his great example of faith, do such a thing? What led to this fateful action? Let's examine a few explanations.

Ignorance

In an episode of the *Andy Griffith Show*, the uncouth mountain man, Ernest T. Bass, was bemoaning the fact that he was "no count." Andy, trying to reassure him, said, "No Ernest T., you are not 'no count'—you are just ignorant!" To which Ernest T. responds, "You're just being nice."

While ignorance is not always a nice thing to attribute to someone, it often played a role in ancient cultural behavior. Generations in the ancient past did not have a proper understanding of genetics. For example, they had no understanding that both the male and female played equal roles in conception. They believed that the male carried the seed and the woman was merely an incubator. With that faulty understanding, one can easily see where this story is headed. If a woman is an incubator, one is as good as another! Viewed in these terms, we can at least understand why both Abraham and Sarah would seek to find the best incubator possible (or at least one that worked!) in order to carry out God's work. Besides, God hadn't said anything about Sarah being the mother of Abraham's offspring.

Influence of Social Pressure

Remember that Abraham and Sarah were living in a pagan culture. Without trying to justify their actions, we must be careful to not expect of them behavior that one should reasonably only expect in a fully developed Christian culture. Infertility was believed to be the punishment for some wrong—and it was primarily the woman's fault. Therefore, enormous social pressure was upon an infertile woman. She was the blunt of ridicule and scorn; such a "wrong" was often grounds for divorce. With the burden of reproduction falling on her, there was tremendous pressure upon a woman to "incubate." Logically, if she couldn't do so herself, then she was responsible for finding someone who could—practicing the ancient version of surrogate motherhood. Sarah broke no social rules with her offer to Abraham. She was well within the acceptable practice of her time. However, just because everyone is doing it doesn't mean God approves.

In today's vernacular, her actions would be called "situational ethics." The term implies that an action is judged right or wrong depending upon the situation. When you believe that you are on a righteous mission and that the ultimate outcome of your actions will be right, you will be tempted to believe that the end will be justified by whatever means you used to accomplish it. This is especially true if you think you have been unfairly treated. (This is an attitude Sarah clearly expressed by "blaming" God for her situation.) Following this line of flawed thinking, as long as you mean well and as long as you want to get the right results, then it doesn't matter how you arrive at the destination.

It could be argued that Sarah's moral conscience was still under development and that her flawed reasoning is common practice given those limitations. That may be true. However, even though Abraham was also under moral and conscience development, he was more responsible than Sarah. Abraham had the advantage of having heard the "Voice" and had experienced firsthand some of the blessings that come from hearing and heeding that Voice. Privilege brings greater responsibility.

Impatience

We all have our secret sins—those things that we have tried to tuck away in the dark recesses of our hidden past. Yet, in spite of all our efforts, secret sin often reemerges at the most inopportune moments. For Abraham, his secret sin seems to be impatience. We've already seen impatience prompt his faithless detour into Egypt. Like prairie dogs that disappear in a hole, only to reappear and bark from another of many holes, so we see impatience reemerging to "bark" again just four chapters later. This episode in Abraham's story reminds us that we must be careful about making quick decisions without considering long-term consequences. There are at least two sources of impatience that we would do well to note.

First, impatience comes from fear. How many times have we been impatient because we feared rejection, so we gave in? We feared we'd never love again, so we "settled" and married someone who was less than our previous standard. We feared we'd never get "this good of a financial deal," so we bought it. In each of these scenarios (and many others, I might add), we live to regret our impatient actions. Could this be the very reason why God had told Abraham, *"Do not be afraid?"* (Genesis 15:1). Could God's words 10 years earlier be intended to head off a possible disaster, knowing the tendency of Abraham's heart to fear?

Second, impatience comes from the need to control. The need to control is actually another form of fear—the fear of not being in control. Abraham didn't like being in a situation that he couldn't control. We've met people like this—we call them control freaks. Such people are usually impatient. Maybe you work for a boss like that, or maybe you live with someone like that or maybe you are like that! Abraham's need to be in control of his situation made him vulnerable to solutions that would prove to be costly and painful later.

In the Midst of Mistakes, Be Careful Not to Make It Worse

Once mistakes are made, things tend to get worse. Notice in Abraham's story how our response to a mistake can exacerbate the situation. There are three "mistaken" responses to our mistakes:

Sarah Pointed Her Finger

*"Then Sarai said to Abram, '**You** are responsible for the wrong I am suffering. I put my servant in your arms, and now that she knows she is pregnant, **she** despises me. May the LORD judge between you and me'"* (Genesis 16:5). Once more reflecting the story of Eve in the Garden of Eden, Sarah quickly looks for someone to blame. She turns on Abraham (and Hagar) and shifts the blame for her failed actions. Abraham would have agreed with a book I once saw entitled, *How to Understand Women*. When you open it, there is nothing but blank pages!

Abraham Rolled His Eyes

"Your servant is in your hands...Do with her whatever you think best" (Genesis 16:6).

When Sarah was letting him have it for going along with her idea, I can imagine that Abraham rolled his eyes. His response for her to do "whatever you think is best" is a typical male response. Actually what he says is Hebrew for, "*Talk to the hand because the head ain't listening!*" At least we discover where the term so commonly used by youth today originates—"*Whatever!*"

Who is supposed to be the leader? Abraham has spent the greatest amount of time with God. As spiritual head of his family, he should have taken positive action to correct the wrong done to Hagar. Instead of taking the lead to address the problems he helped to create, he tries to dodge his responsibility and the situation grows worse.

Hagar Checked Out

"*Then Sarai mistreated Hagar; so she fled from her...'I'm running away from my mistress Sarai,' she answered*" (Genesis 6a, 8b). We would be hard pressed to lay upon Hagar any fault in this particular incident. No, Hagar was not perfect. Like all of us, she had her own sins. But Hagar did not create the situation she was forced to endure. That being said, Hagar's fault, if it must be given, lies in her response to this unfolding crisis. Faced with painful circumstances, Hagar checks out and calls it quits. She flees into the desert in hopes of outrunning the problems she has left behind.

We see this Hagar-approach to pain in the wake of many failures and problems today. Hagar's tendency to run from trouble is not unlike those who often change locations. Even though they may not be totally at fault with a trying situation, rather than working to change it, they choose to change addresses. Changing addresses may mean changing jobs, or changing churches or even changing spouses. I've seen church members take the Hagar way out. I've known pastors like Hagar as well.

Sometimes you don't even have to physically leave to check out. I know some couples that are married, yet emotionally they've already checked out. Although they would never admit it, they have already divorced. I think about the ones who have checked out with the aid of addicting substances. Suicide is the ultimate checkout. While we are all prone to mistakes, we must be careful that we don't make our failure into more than it is. Once we mess up, we must beware of making matters worse.

Follow the Steps to Make It Right

It means a lot to me to know that in the midst of all this chaos, God not only sees my situation but He also steps *into* my situation. Having fled into the wilderness, an angel of the Lord finds Hagar (Genesis 16:7-13). There is good reason to believe that this "Angel of the Lord" was, in fact, a pre-incarnate visit of our Lord Jesus. Imagine the exciting implications! In the midst of her pain and loneliness and failure, Jesus shows up! How much like Jesus to show up when we need encouragement. How much like Jesus to focus time and attention on a poor young girl (and not a man of renown and wealth like Abraham). How much like Jesus to come to a foreigner, a servant in a strange land. How much like Jesus to come to a failure who had been a part of a bad mistake.

We can take great comfort that our Lord shows Himself to be a Friend of the friendless, a Savior of sinners. When you think no one cares for you, just remember Hagar. He is looking for you!

The rest of her story and the encounter with the Angel show us that when mistakes are made, there are certain steps we must follow to correct the situation.

Step One: *Assume responsibility (v.8a)*

The word "repentance" is never used in this story. However, this is what Hagar did. Having met the Lord in a dramatic, life-changing moment, Hagar "turns around." Hagar's change of direction is not unlike one who truly repents and changes the course of his or her life. And having met the Lord, we are not allowed to evade responsible action. It is true that God can mend together the pieces of our broken situations, but we must also assume responsibility for the part we've played. God issued two questions to alter Hagar's course and turn her back to the place of responsible action (v.8).

- *"Where have you come from?"(What led to this mess and how did it happen?)*
- *"Where are you going?" (If you continue on the path you are on, where will you end up?)*

Think about your answer to these questions. Your answer to the first question will ensure that you will not return to this same place again by the same path. Not understanding how we got where we are only means that we are doomed to repeat whatever actions got us into our mess in the first place! The second question is just as important: *"Where are you going?"* In other words, "If you continue in this behavior, where will it take you?"

Step Two: *Be accountable to those in authority (v.9)*
No one likes to submit. We see it as weakness. But that's pride talking, and the Bible teaches that pride always comes before destruction (Proverbs 16:18). God explained that it was important for Hagar to submit to the people God placed in authority over her. Like Hagar, we will resist submitting to God at some point in our lives. However, authority is also one of the ways we work our way back from mistakes. In the wake of failure, it is important that we have authority figures that will hold us accountable for healthy habits and correct processes. For example, if you are working your way back from

professional failure, an experienced life-coach might be in order. If you are returning from a failure in marriage and need to rebuild trust, a caring and knowledgeable counselor or pastor would be helpful. Regardless of your circumstances, returning to authority and submitting to those over you will teach you valuable life lessons, just like Hagar.

Step Three: *Align with the Word of God (vv. 11, 15)*
Upon returning from a bad situation, be careful to align your future actions with God's Word. Having been given a specific directive (to return to Abraham and Sarah, to have the baby and to name him Ishmael), Hagar is prompt to obey. We are not given a long explanation surrounding her return to carry her baby to term—we are just told in verse 15 that she bore Abraham a son and gave him the name Ishmael. Life is back on track. In the same way, prompt obedience will help ensure our own full recovery—even from the worst of mistakes.

Life Lessons from Silence

This story leaves us pondering some key life principles that we should include in our backpacks as we journey along our trail of transforming faith. Hagar's story is ancillary to Abraham's, but it is no less important. While we may be encouraged by the lessons from this lesser character, the larger story of Abraham's affair with her is more difficult to process. At its most basic level, it is simply a sober reminder of how weak we are in times of silence. It is difficult to gain complete victory over the hidden sins that continue to plague us long after we begin our faith journey—especially when we don't sense God actively at work in our lives. For Abraham, the test of silence revealed that his faith was still under construction. This would be the case for his entire life.

As difficult as this situation with Hagar was, there was still one more test Abraham would face on his journey. It would require every ounce of strength to pass, and it would teach Abraham more about himself and his God than he ever dreamed possible. This final test begins at the foothills of Mt. Moriah and takes Abraham all the way up to the pinnacle of transformation, a transformation of faith.

Trailnotes

- In the midst of silence, we long to hear a voice of direction. Be careful about the voices you follow!

- Don't try to push God out of His silence—stay still and trust. Why is it difficult to be patient amid God's silence?

- Never allow your situation and the pressures you feel to dictate your moral response.

- Everyone makes mistakes. Assuming responsibility, submitting to authority and following God's Word will enable us to set things straight.

- The choices we make today have consequences that will shape our lives (and the lives of others!) tomorrow.

CHAPTER 10

The Final Test

"When they reached the place
God had told him about,
Abraham built an altar there
and arranged the wood on
it. He bound his son Isaac
and laid him on the altar,
on top of the wood. Then he
reached out his hand and took
the knife to slay his son..."
(Genesis 22:9-10)

In the early morning hours of May 2, 2011, a U.S. Naval Special Warfare Group (SEAL Team Six), would execute a plan that had started in September the previous year and would ultimately test the full resources of the U.S. military and intelligence communities. "Operation Neptune Spear" was based on information from U.S. intelligence sources that indicated the whereabouts of the most wanted fugitive of the United States. Instead of being stowed away in a remote cave, Osama bin Laden was actually hiding out in an isolated compound located on eight acres in Pakistan. The SEALS' mission was to either capture or kill him for masterminding the September 11, 2001 terror strikes on U.S. soil.

To prepare for this critical moment, a detailed mockup of bin Laden's compound had been built in two U.S. locations to simulate the exact anticipated conditions. This secret raid would require months of intensive training, meticulous intelligence gathering, and tens of millions of dollars. Although the raid on bin Laden's compound was 10 years in the making, the test itself would last for only 38 minutes. The critical moments that unfolded in the darkness that final early morning in 2011 were the result of many years of exhaustive research and grueling physical training. U.S. military and intelligence groups would champion this test a success after these words relayed from one of the SEALS, "Geronimo EKIA" (Enemy Killed In Action).

Likewise, what will unfold in the remaining critical moments of Abraham's story will be the fruit of many years of preparation. The events that unfold for Abraham on a remote mountain in Salem would be the final test of faith in a long journey. He would be asked to build an altar on Mt. Moriah in order to sacrifice his beloved son, Isaac. *"Then God said, 'Take your son, your only son, Isaac, whom you love, and go to the region of Moriah. Sacrifice him there as a burnt offering on one of the mountains I will tell you about'"* (Genesis 22:2). Abraham had no clue what lay ahead for him, but the results of this test would influence all future generations.

Testing or Tempting?

Final exams can be painful. For years after graduating from seminary, I had a reoccurring dream where I was back in seminary taking a final exam for which I was totally unprepared. (Maybe it wasn't a dream at all. Perhaps it was the like the preacher who dreamed he was preaching and woke up only to discover that it was true!) Abraham was not unprepared for this final exam—in fact, everything in his life to that point had prepared him for this moment.

The exam that Abraham faced would constitute the most severe test that any servant of God would ever face. It was clearly designed as a test, but tests are not the same as temptations. *Tests* are the means whereby God reveals our worth and strength (primarily for us to see!). On the other hand, *temptations* come from Satan with a destructive intent. However, in our minds, the two may not be clearly distinguishable at the time.

James wrote in the New Testament, *"No one should say, 'God is tempting me.' For God cannot be tempted by evil, nor does he tempt anyone"* (James 1:13). God does not entice us to do evil. Therein is the difference: temptation is the enticement of Satan intended to destroy or disrupt our fellowship with God; tests are given by God to develop our faith and prove our strength. It is a statement of God's sovereignty that He can take the same set of circumstances that Satan intends for our destruction and use it for our good (Romans 8:28). For this reason, the same circumstance can be both a test and a temptation. Both Satan and God can use a single event for totally different purposes. Satan can use a particular matter to disrupt our faith and bring discouragement. In comparison, God can use that same situation to stretch our faith and draw us closer to Him. Paul says, "...*God is faithful; he will not let you be tempted beyond what you can bear. But when you are tempted, he will also provide a way out so that you can stand up under it*" (1 Corinthians 10:13). What better way for God to stretch our faith than to prove our success over tempting circumstances?

What is about to unfold on a remote mountainside altar will teach Abraham something about himself and his God that will impact the course of human history. And, in the process, Abraham will teach us some valuable insights regarding worship.

The Perfect Time for Testing

The opening sentence of Chapter 22 in Genesis sets the context for this final exam with great simplicity: "*Some time later...*" Within that time, God had already prepared Abraham for what he was about to face (which leads us to another crucial difference between a test and a temptation). God desires that we be successful, and the tests He designs are intended for that purpose. Satan, on the other hand, designs temptations to lead us to failure. That is why temptations will often come during periods in our lives that make it more likely for us to fail—times of stress, loneliness, physical exhaustion and discouragement. Satan knows when to hit us at our most vulnerable moments for his advantage.

However, God's tests usually come after we have rested and our energy is replenished so that we are ready. When we last left Abraham at the end of Genesis 21, we find Abraham in a state of physical rest and spiritual strength. "*Abraham planted a tamarisk tree in Beersheba, and there he called upon the name of the Lord, the Eternal God*" (21:33). Tamarisk trees were planted for their shade. There in the shade of his newly planted tree, Abraham communed with his God. Life was good. He and Sarah had finally had their son, Isaac—the long-awaited heir that would make Abraham the father of many nations. He was probably in his late teens, early twenties, when the story in Genesis 22 took place.

For the first time, we are told that Abraham viewed God as "Eternal" (21:33). The word means "unchanging…without end…everlasting." It's not a coincidence that immediately following this spiritual period in his life, Abraham's theology would be sorely tested. Mark it down—there will come a time when your view of God will be put to the test. Abraham is about to be challenged with an earthly decision that will have eternal dimensions. The relaxing scene of a shade tree is about to be shattered two verses later with the words, "… *Some time later God tested Abraham.*"

How quickly life can change! In one moment, Abraham was sipping lemonade under the tamarisk tree; in the next moment, the walls of his carefree, pleasant life come crashing down. Storms can brew quickly. This is as true for a person of faith as it is for a pagan. Faith does not immunize us against such moments. A person of faith can experience violent shifts as anyone else can do. We are not immune. Neither are we amused. Such times often confuse us and make us wonder if God is cruel and doesn't love us. Remember that such times have a dual purpose—they can unravel us, or they can reveal the depth of our commitment to God. The choice is ours to make.

Worship Begins with a Perspective

The test Abraham faces on Mt. Moriah is primarily a test of worship, but it begins here in Beersheba with Abraham finally securing a proper view of God. The Eternal God must also be our "Lord" (21:33). We must be in relationship with the Eternal God and desire to submit to Him in all things. What is ultimately practiced at Moriah must begin with the perspective found at Beersheba. Worship requires a perspective of mental and spiritual alignment that sees the Eternal God as Lord.

True worship is not about us...it's about God. However, we often try to make it about us. When we talk of worship styles and preferences and allow those preferences to determine the extent or worth of our worship, we make it all about us. We become like religious consumers with our shopping carts and list. We go to church looking to fill up our carts with something that meets our felt needs. That is why most religious consumers will select a church (or leave a church!) more on music than theology. It doesn't matter so much how biblically sound the preaching is to a religious consumer; it's more about whether the music meets their taste or the children and youth programs meet their "needs." A consumer will trade sound theology for something that will make them feel good. God help us!

Jesus said, "*It is more blessed to give than to receive*" (Acts 20:35). However, religious consumers don't go to church to *give*; they go primarily to *get*. We miss out on the blessings when our focus is on receiving. Ironically, when we go to church primarily to get, we don't receive much. God reminds us through Abraham that worship is all about Him. Abraham will put his eternal perspective of God into an everyday practice of surrender. For Abraham, it was all about the Eternal God, his Lord.

Worship Requires Preparation

On a cold, clear January morning in 2003, US Airways Express flight 5481 was preparing for takeoff from Charlotte-Douglas International Airport. The flight was destined for Greenville/Spartanburg, a short 100 miles away. At the controls of the aircraft was twenty-five-year-old Katie Leslie, along with 19 passengers and two crewmembers. As the jet accelerated down runway 18R, it lifted off; but 37 seconds into the flight, witnesses reported the jet pitched sharply before it seemed to stall and veer backward to the airport. Flight 5481 crashed into a nearby hangar, killing all persons on board.

The National Transportation Safety Board immediately began their investigation. The maintenance records were scrutinized, going back to a maintenance facility in West Virginia. The NTSB found evidence of prior problems with attachment bolts for the vertical stabilizer. In fact, the jet had a record of service difficulties 10 times prior to the crash. The real tragedy of this event is that it didn't have to happen. Proper maintenance could have prevented it.

Likewise, it is vital that our spiritual maintenance record be up-to-date. We may think that we are flying pretty high, but if our maintenance is careless and we overlook critical areas, we may also lose the spiritual altitude of worship. Thankfully, that didn't happen with Abraham. Before that worshipful scene at Moriah unfolds, there were at least two forms of spiritual preparations that were set in place.

1. Abraham's obedience was immediate. *("Early the next morning..." 22:3)*
Evidently, Abraham had received the message to sacrifice his son sometime in the night. The news must have awakened him in a cold sweat. What was he to make of this? Could he have misunderstood? Should he tell Sarah? Oh, the questions that must have filled his panicked mind! However, the record indicates that in spite of his torturous thoughts, he quietly and resolutely went about obeying the word that had come to him. The obedience of Abraham was remarkable in that he showed himself:

- **Willing to *do* the unthinkable**. (v.2) *"Take your son...sacrifice him there as a burnt offering"*

- **Willing to *go* to the unknown** (v.3) *"...go to... one of the mountains I will tell you about"*

- **Willing to *give* the unlimited** (v.9) *"When they reached the place God had told him about, Abraham...bound his son Isaac and laid him on the altar..."*

These are the same requirements of true worship for us. We must be willing to obey the Word of God at all costs. Anything less is worthless.

2. Abraham's faith was immovable. *("On the third day Abraham looked up and saw the place in the distance. He said to his servants, 'Stay here with the donkey while I and the boy go over there. We will worship and then we will come back to you.'" vv. 4-5)*
Having set out on his heartbreaking quest for "the place,"

136

Abraham would find himself again following a call to an uncertain destination. This is strangely reminiscent of an earlier, unspecified calling that he received from God to leave Haran (12:1). Abraham was getting good at following God's directions. It reflected a growth in faith. This present journey, however, would test that faith beyond measure.

For the two days' journey, Abraham's heart must have been breaking beyond imagination. For two days, he must have been numb with immeasurable pain and shock. We are not told how he knew this was "*the place*" on the third day, but the fact that Abraham was God's friend made him sensitive to the divine directions that come from such intimacy. Abraham's Friend didn't have to say anything. Abraham knew His heart.

Which is Harder: Trust or Obey?

Abraham's faith remained immovable even in the face of what appeared to be a major contradiction of God's character. In this particular incidence, God's promises seemed to contradict His commands. How could God fulfill His promises to Abraham if Isaac was dead? It made no sense! If you were faced with a similar situation, what would you do?

The unfolding of this drama underscores the truth that trusting God is life's most difficult challenge. In fact, trusting God is harder than obeying God. Obedience is worked out within well-defined boundaries of God's revealed will. In His Word, God reveals what is expected of us. That's not to say that carrying out His will is always easy. It's usually not. But at least we have a clear direction if we choose to follow it.

Faith, on the other hand, is another matter. Faith

is worked out in an arena with no boundaries. We are often left in the dark as to the purpose and duration of adverse circumstances. We obey what we know; we are often forced to trust what we don't understand. That is what makes Abraham's faith so remarkable! When we disobey, we defy His authority. When we doubt, we question His goodness.

Abraham could not doubt the goodness of God. Even in the face of apparent contradiction, Abraham believed God would be true to His promises. In a remarkable statement of faith, Abraham expresses his confidence in God when he says that he and the boy would come back after the sacrifice of worship (v.5). The writer of Hebrews 11 comments on this remarkable faith: *"By faith Abraham, when God tested him, offered Isaac as a sacrifice. He who had received the promises was about to sacrifice his one and only son, even though God had said to him, 'It is through Isaac that your offspring will be reckoned.' Abraham reasoned that God could raise the dead, and figuratively speaking, he did receive Isaac back from death"* (vv.17-19).

Abraham trusted God to do something that He had never done before. In order to be true to His promises, God would have to raise Isaac back from the dead. This feat required an immovable faith in a God who had proven Himself reliable in Abraham's colorful past.

Worship requires no less from us. We trust Him as our Eternal God, and in so doing, we trust that whatever He allows into our lives has an eternal purpose for us. Now we may see through a glass darkly, but by faith we know that one day what we have been allowed to endure will gain for us the fulfillment of His eternal promises (1 Corinthians 13:12).

Worship Demands Priority

The first occurrence in the Bible of both the words "*love*" (v.2) and "*worship*" (v.5) occur in this story. Abraham is told, almost mockingly, to "*Take your son, your only son, Isaac, whom you love, and…sacrifice him*" (v.2). True worship always requires what we love. Worship requires that we give our "Isaac" as an act of sacrifice as well. In order to do that, we must identify what our Isaac is.

Our Isaac may be our greatest love

Jesus restated a requirement of God since the days of Moses when he said, "*Love the Lord your God with all your heart and with all your soul and with all your mind*" (Matthew 22:37). God will tolerate no rivals with His love. The first of God's Ten Commandments states clearly, "*You shall have no other gods before me*" (Exodus 20:3). The word "*before*" in Hebrew means "*before my face*" or "*in my presence.*" Think about it: How big is the face of an omnipresent God? Pretty big, wouldn't you say? God is not saying, "I want to be your number one." God is saying, "I want to be your *only* one!" God says to Abraham, "I want your total, unshared love."

Isaac was the son Abraham prayed for earnestly for 100 years. There is no question that Abraham treasured Isaac above any earthly thing. The question was, had he elevated Isaac to a place above any spiritual being? If you or I love anything more than we love God—child, spouse, parent, popularity, comfort, career aspirations or financial security—anything—then that is our Isaac and it must be placed on the altar. God demands our supreme love. He will tolerate nothing less.

Our Isaac may be the source of our greatest joy

The name "Isaac" means "laughter." Would you be willing

to sacrifice the thing that brings joy and laughter into your life? Would you be willing to put to death the thing that makes you smile, or brings a sense of fulfillment? God wants to be the source of our pleasure.

Our Isaac may be our greatest gift from God

It is an inherent flaw in humanity to focus upon the gifts, to the exclusion of the Giver. Isaac was the greatest gift from God that Abraham had ever received. In requiring Isaac back, God tested Abraham to see if he was responsible enough to handle His blessing.

God cannot trust us sometimes with His blessings. Some of the most dangerous things that come in our lives are blessings from God. For example, we may be gifted with the ability to make money—but what if the money we make becomes an idol for us? That's dangerous. I know of singers (and preachers!) who have the ability to emotionally sway an audience. Such a skill is a gift of God. Sadly, I've also known of such individuals who slowly started turning away from God as the source of their skill and began depending on their own personality and charisma. In such situations, it is not unusual that God would allow the stream of blessings to dry up in order to drive that person back to the true source of his or her blessings.

How often has God given us a blessing, only to have that blessing weaken our devotion to Him? God may give us things only to have those gifts crowd out our faith and devotion to the Giver. I have found that some of the greatest barriers to trusting God were some of God's greatest blessings in my life when those blessings became the object of my faith and devotion. The Chinese evangelist Watchman Nee once wrote about Isaac, "[He] represents many gifts of God's grace. Before God gives them, our hands are empty. Afterwards they are full. Sometimes God reaches out his hand to take ours in fellowship. Then we need an empty hand to put into his. But when we have received his gifts and are nursing them to ourselves, our hands are full, and when God puts out his hand we have no empty hand for him. At such a time, we must let go of the gifts that fill our hands so that we can take the hand of God...Isaac can be done without, but God is eternal."[11]

God Will Provide

We now come to that sacred moment when Abraham will bind and place his son on that crudely made altar. There is no hint that he bound Isaac because he resisted. This weakened old man could not have imposed his will upon Isaac, who was by now a strong, young man. The binding seems to be more about Abraham than Isaac. Perhaps it was to ensure that his shaky hand would find its mark as humanely as possible. As Abraham places his knife on the throat of this tender sacrifice, his trembling hand is suddenly stopped. *"But the angel of the LORD called out to him from heaven, 'Abraham! Abraham!' 'Here I am,' he replied. 'Do not lay a hand on the boy,' he said. 'Do not do anything to him. Now I know that you fear God, because you have not withheld from me your son, your only son'"* (22:10-12).

God has seen enough. The full intentions of this servant of God have been made obvious. It is clear there is no limit to the extent to which this servant would go to trust God. There was no need to continue this test. Abraham had passed. At that moment, he heard the nearby bleating of a ram caught in a thicket. God had

---

11   Watchman Nee, *Changed into His Likeness*, Christian Literature Crusade, 1967, p.62.

provided a substitute sacrifice. Isaac was spared.

It's hard to imagine the impressions that this episode left with Abraham and others. What would Isaac remember of this event? How would this shape his opinion of his father? What about Sarah? Did she ever know what happened on this six-day absence? Did Abraham ever dare to tell her? And what about Abraham himself? Jesus may have answered that last question in John 8:56, "...*Your father Abraham rejoiced at the thought of seeing my day; he saw it and was glad.*"

What was it that Abraham saw? It is not beyond reason that Abraham saw this event as a dress rehearsal for another act of sacrifice yet to come. He would have no way of knowing that it would be upon this very hill that God would one day demonstrate His supreme love for all humanity through the willing sacrifice of His beloved Son. What God had prevented Abraham from doing, God would willingly endure for the sake of all. Perhaps Abraham saw love so divine that it was willing to endure such a loss. Perhaps Abraham saw an innocent sacrifice, entangled by the sins of the world, laid upon another altar to appease a holy and righteous God. Perhaps Abraham even saw the resurrection of that slain sacrifice—the real act of which Abraham had received only in symbol. Yes, Abraham "rejoiced" as he departed that mountain scene. The trail for Abraham had been long and difficult. But through it all, his faith had been transformed. Yes, Abraham rejoiced at what he had learned of God—and what he had learned about himself.

The End of the Trail

At the foot of one of the Swiss Alps is a marker honoring a man who fell to his death attempting a climb. The marker gives his name and this brief epitaph: "He died climbing." The epitaph of every Christian should be that they died climbing the upward trail toward an Eternal God. This is the trail of faith. Abraham traveled this trail, as you and I must also do—though it is fraught with many challenges and even failures. Like Abraham, we journey alongside the Eternal God whom Abraham trusted as a Friend—a Friend that transformed his life. No one who walks this trail of faith remains the same. It is a trail that will transform our lives as well. We may die climbing, but we *live* by faith.

Trailnotes

- At the time, we can't easily identify whether or not our circumstances are trials or temptations. How we respond, however, will often declare which kind it was!

- Trials will often come after periods of rest and renewal. Temptations will often come when we are the most vulnerable.

- Obeying God is not always easy, but it is usually worked out in well-defined boundaries of what we know. Faith, on the other hand, is worked out in an arena with no boundaries when we do not understand.

- The true test of worship is our willingness to give our "Isaac" back to God. What is your "Isaac" and how willing are you to surrender that to God?

31057731R00087

Made in the USA
Lexington, KY
28 March 2014